CRITICAL ACCLAIM FOR CAROLE HYATT'S BOOKS

When Smart People Fail: Building Yourself for Success
(co-authored with Linda Gottleib)

"A fail-safe system of protective thinking that guards against the personal malfunctioning failure can cause...the title should read: 'What People Who Fail Do *If* They're Smart'."

THE WASHINGTON POST

"An upbeat, *practical* book about how to use failure as a springboard for success."

DONNA SHALALA, SECRETARY
DEPT. OF HEALTH & HUMAN SERVICES

"Like many of the subjects in the book, I've made mistakes, I've learned from them and now I've moved on. Hyatt and Gottleib confirm that that is the best way to deal with losing. What a relief."

GERALDINE A. FERRARO

"Should be thoroughly enjoyed by so many highly intelligent and hard-driven people...who have a difficult time in reaching their goals. It will give them encouragement to get over their failures and see the new opportunities that are there for them to discover."

J. PETER GRACE, CHAIRMAN & CEO
W.R. GRACE & COMPANY

"Their detailed prescriptions will prove comforting to anyone newly wounded and bleeding from a failure."

THE NEW YORK TIMES

Shifting Gears: Mastering Career Change

"For millions of Americans, Carole Hyatt's *Shifting Gears* arrived none too soon, for career change has become a way of life...This book provides hope and valuable guidance both for those in need of emergency help and for the many others who are stuck in the doldrums of their life's voyage...Through *Shifting Gears,* one can learn to know oneself, to explore one's possibilities, and to make those possibilities real...I think it will rank as a classic, along with *What Color Is Your Parachute?*"

THOMAS R. HORTON, CHAIRMAN AND CEO
AMERICAN MANAGEMENT ASSOCIATION

"In the next decade and beyond, the common wisdom has it that most of us will have several substantial career changes. Carole Hyatt's book will be an invaluable tool for the millions of people who will be 'shifting gears' and going into career-change overdrive in these changing times."

HARVEY MACKAY, AUTHOR OF *SWIM WITH THE SHARKS WITHOUT BEING EATEN ALIVE* AND *BEWARE OF THE NAKED MAN WHO OFFERS YOU HIS SHIRT*

"Shifting Gears deals very effectively with two of our greatest challenges: changes and finding a career that we enjoy. For many it is sure to be the light that dispels the darkness."

WALLY AMOS, FOUNDER OF FAMOUS AMOS COOKIES

"Hyatt's examples aren't merely inspiring; they help readers see the obstacles to making a major change and determining whether they have what it takes to orchestrate a career make over."

U.S. NEWS & WORLD REPORT

"Hyatt has an uncanny knack for illuminating the realities people face in today's job market and helping you recognize who you are, in the context of the job market, and acting on that knowledge."

CHICAGO TRIBUNE

LIFETIME EMPLOYABILITY

To Paul —
How good to
meet you —
You come well
heralded —
Love your synthesis —

Love

Carole Hyatt — 10/25/95

LIFETIME EMPLOYABILITY

HOW TO BECOME INDISPENSABLE

CAROLE HYATT

MASTERMEDIA LIMITED
NEW YORK

Designed by Michael Woyton
Manufactured in the United States of America
10 9 8 7

DEDICATION

This book is in memory of Annie May Walker-Johnson who, with a third-grade education, taught our family the true meaning of service and work commitment.

ACKNOWLEDGEMENTS

I want to thank Connie deSwaan for her professionalism, organization and creativity in the preparation of this book.

To Lynda Lampert for her assistance and the lesson she has taught me about positive attitude.

To Susan Stautberg for her editorial ideas and stewardship.

Many thanks to Richard Malevat and Emma Palzere for their intelligent transcriptions and computer know-how.

To the hundreds of men and women who were so generous with their interview time, invaluable insights and advice. Some have allowed their names to be used and others have asked to remain anonymous, as indicated by an asterisk by their name. Their contributions are the heart of this book and I am very grateful.

CONTENTS

PREFACE

W hen I first began my career in the outplacement industry, more than 15 years ago, I and those I counseled could have profited greatly from a book like *Lifetime Employability*. In the 1970s and 1980s outplacement counselors were engaged by corporations to "ease their conscience" and help the separated employee find new employment. Much of counselor's time was spent helping the unemployed to rebuild their confidence and self-esteem and to teach them job search techniques. Today, the circumstances are different. Outplacement firms are engaged not only to help employees find new jobs and rebuild self-esteem, but to help those very same employees build and create a future in the new "work place." Gone are the days where the end result was measured by having the candidate land a job. Today we strive to equip the unemployed with strategies necessary to survive in both a growing economy or, like today, perhaps a fluctuating one.

Yesterday, my colleagues and I helped those in managing change; today we help them in mastering and profiting from change.

While there are many indications that today "corporate change" is slowing down and unemployment rates are decreasing, the fact remains that change of some sort will always continue. The process of cutting staff has been known as downsizing and many organizations have done it several times. No industry or organization has been immune. In fact, major Fortune 500 companies announce two years ahead that they plan to cut jobs. Not only are permanent jobs becoming scarce, but those vacant ones often pay 10-50 percent less than such positions paid only a few years ago and may demand a relocation.

Often the process of building the new organization has been dubbed re-engineering. For several years the downsized employee used the traditional methods of landing a job: ads, networking, search firms, and yet continued to be downsized out of the corporations. Today, the downsized employee or the actively employed individual faces the new millennium with the need to re-engineer himself/herself for the future and for survival. Job search methods or survival techniques for the re-engineered employee are and will not follow into the traditional methods. The new paradigm of employment in the re-engineered work place will require emphasis of self-marketing and self-employability.

What talents will set the employable apart from the crowd? My colleagues and I agree that having many talents will set an individual apart from the crowd. Cross-training, cross-learning and transferable skills, often the buzzwords for the 70s and 80s, have become the requirements of the 90s. Continuing education or re-education will keep an individual employable, but not necessarily full time at the same employer. Since contingency employment arrangements will become the norm and no longer the exception, flexibility and mobility will be critical elements for success.

The outplaced individual of yesterday often asked me or my colleagues, "Why didn't I see it coming? How can I prevent it from happening again? What are new rules and why didn't someone tell me that they have changed? Who can tell me which of my skills will be most marketable in the future?" Today the most sophisticated ask, "How can I prevent myself from being in 'Corporate Bondage' again? How can I purchase a career insurance policy? Who will underwrite it? How do I write a proposal for service? What type of contract do I need for a project? What accounting software package should I use in my business? How do I negotiate advertising fees?"

In a recent survey of outplacement candidates in the United States, we have found that close to 20 percent launch into entrepreneurial activities. The number rises each year and will continue to rise as corporations embrace the re-engineered workforce. My colleagues in Canada agree and have indicated that perhaps 30 percent of their candidates seek out entrepreneurial activities. What does it take to buy an insurance policy emphasizing values, interest, and balance? Successful job seekers will view themselves as "contractors" whether they take the entrepreneurial route or employment route. Even those with full-time corporate jobs will view themselves not as an employee with a boss, but as a self-employed company with a client and an ill-defined length of contract.

Recent job development statistics indicate that jobs are being created in the small business arena and not in corporations. Are we returning to an era where each man and woman was the master of their own destiny and he/she owned it? Yes, today's worker must be his/her own firm, and his/her own employer. The successful job seekers must forge ahead in analyzing their marketable skills, targeting their markets and selling their services. Advertising one's capabilities will be the norm, not the exception. Staff recruiters will soon become purchasing agents.

The new job seeker unlike his predecessor will find once again joy in the work place. Each job of tomorrow will be based on one's interest, skills, abilities and ownership. Teambuilding won't be taught or trained; it will be a way of doing business and will be inherent in the virtual office. The traditional workplace will be history and the new paradigm will survive.

How does one prepare for the new paradigm and break out of the traditional mold of planning one's career and developing winning schemes? *Lifetime Employability* provides a sound footing for those preparing and working within the re-engineered workplace. It teaches the new rules and dispels the myths. It puts the job seeker on the Information Highway and maps the routes for life's journey to productive and satisfactory employment. Read it, study it, embrace it!

JOHN POYNTON
President, Association of Outplacement
Consulting Firms International

INTRODUCTION

Ye shall know the truth and the truth shall make ye mad," wrote author Aldous Huxley. If you picked up this book, the truth that may be making you mad is that the work place—as you knew it —keeps changing under your feet and you're not quite sure where you stand in the job market.

One of six issues may be the real crux of your dilemma:

➤ You're seeking the secret of job security to make sure you never lose the job you hold now.

➤ Although your current situation may not be immediately due for change, your perspective may be. You want to be prepared.

➤ You feel like a "victim of organizational change"—your company has just merged or been downsized, and each day brings you closer to the news of how you will fare in the new management.

➤ You've held the same job for eight or 10 years, and your company has changed. Now you need to adjust your point of view from industrial age thinking to information age thinking and you feel a bit panicked.

➤ You're dissatisfied with the company you're with and your prospects for promotion, you feel stuck there and unsure of where else to go and who might employ you.

➤ You're approaching 35 or 40 years old, or older, and wonder how employable you'll seem to potential employers, what kind of job you'd be offered and how to best sell yourself.

All these concerns hinge, in various degrees, on the shape the current marketplace has taken—but much more important, how well you can adapt to and thrive in the changes!

What exactly is happening?

Today, the business world is internationally competitive, driven by advanced technology, mass accessibility of information and knowledgeable customers. The mammoth hierarchical organizations we once sought to work for, such IBM, no longer call the shots and are facing their own vulnerability. The effects of such change ripple into every corner of every company.

A *U.S. News & World Report* editorial reported that "some 66 percent of Americans say they worry more about keeping their jobs today than they did two years ago" and that the unease "arises from a dramatic and unique change in the nature of employment." Specifically, they mean that white collar employment no longer provides job security because downsizing and restructuring in companies, large and small, have become a fact of life.

And that introduces the greater truth, one you can do something about: In the new world of work and business, it is the willingness to accept personal freedom and responsibility for yourself that's important. You need to bring integrity and added value to each job you take. It is the skills that you can sell from employer to employer—not a lifetime job with one employer—that confer security.

Today, you are less whom you work for than what you can do. The only constant in this economic market is your commitment to keeping your antenna finely tuned and your skills updated and enhanced.

If your antenna is up, you'll get a number of clear signals from the global market as well as from your company or the industry that interests you. The signals will be either rumors of change or actual change that provide you with information—such as influencing trends or how an industry, or your company, is going and what they'll need from employers or outsourcers.

Once you have the information and accept it, you can figure out how to adapt, respond to the opportunities that change always brings and benefit from it. "Progress always masquerades as trouble," someone said, but it's up to you to fight for the next opportunity—real progress—not for what is on the way out, real trouble. It's during a time of transition that the most and best opportunities exist. Seize them!

You may say, "I don't want to hear about new opportunities. I just want to stay with the job I have."

Understandable. It's hard to let go of what's familiar and what provides us with a profession and a living. However, to stay in this 21st century market, you must reassess your beliefs about change, adaptability and the importance in moving forward. And thus the third truth: You may be getting paid by a company, but you are actually working for yourself. Therefore, you must be responsible for your career and the depth of your work life.

Thus this book. *Lifetime Employability* is both a guide through the mysteries of the business universe brought down to earth and a handbook to help you evaluate your attitudes, your skills and your goals. This book is designed to increase your staying power, become alert to opportunities and be realistic about your situation and your options.

I've interviewed nearly 200 men and women, from coast to coast, whose lives have changed because their jobs or goals have shifted. Many were able to stay with their companies through new management and new structures while others were re-energized by working in another position. All were surprised at how successfully they made a transition to the next step—a step they never dreamed they'd be taking professionally. I spoke to many experts in the field of outplacement, career management, psychology, economics, marketing and sales, and industry forecasters. They all contributed focus and ideas to help me best advise you.

The information in *Lifetime Employability* should trigger new thoughts and actions, bring you to new realizations and revelations about your past and your future. You are the only person who can make decisions for yourself about your career. It is my hope that some of the strategies for adapting to this marketplace will be easy, "make sense" adjustments or confirmations of what you are already successfully doing.

As you read each chapter, you'll be able to clarify how trends in the marketplace have affected you and how companies are run; how methods of working are shifting—such as, the move from championing the "Lone Ranger" to an emphasis on teams and teamwork.

You'll be able to understand where your strengths are, how you can adapt skills or add to them and move up or move on. You'll grasp which personality-fueled attitudes you need to shed and which to adopt to add to your employability.

If there is a metaphor for work and career, then it must be the handmade tapestry—woven from various strands. Each strand represents a facet of your abilities and personality. One strand would be your skills, another your competencies, yet others, your hobbies, experiences, schooling; the trends and opportunities affecting your career; your temperament, adaptability and networks.

As each of us weaves these strands to create the tapestry of our work life, each of us winds up with a different pattern. The unique blend of strands we call "our tapestry," will create a design—for some, it will be more tightly woven and more complicated, and for others, more loosely woven with a broader, more abstract pattern. And remember, you have the ability to continually add strands and change the design.

Most of all, feel confident about your skills, the pleasure you can derive from work and in creating the tapestry of your work life and fulfilling your ambitions in an ever-changing world marketplace.

"If you would prepare for the future, prepare to be surprised."

KENNETH BOULDING,
Futurist

1

STAYING IN—
WHAT IT TAKES TODAY

"No more prizes for predicting rain. Prizes only for building arks."

LOUIS GERSTNER, JR., *CEO, IBM*

Dee Archer*, a 39-year-old Bostonian with Olympian energy and a legendary optimistic disposition, surprised me when I asked her what she thought the average person in the work force needed to stay employable. "Know the computer and never get old!" she said.

These two commodities—the acquisition of continuously updated technological skills and a miracle of nature—sounded a lot like similar plaints I'd listened to recently: What does the work force hold for professionals and mid- and upper-management people 40 and older? What will the future look like for them?

Dee's full story soon explained her unexpected cynicism. A week earlier, Dee cashed her last company check which represented a four-year meteoric career in advertising sales following a management position in publishing. With her native communications skills, gutsiness and brilliant marketing mind, Dee found her niche with a small agency in which she hoped to be made a partner. It nearly happened. A number of false strategic steps coupled by the collapse of their three strongest accounts struck the first death knell for the agency.

---

* All asterisked names throughout this book indicate name changes to protect the interviewee's privacy.

Dee held on for a year, but it became clear that putting the "fat" back on that agency's bare bones was a losing battle, and no longer to her taste. And while the agency needed a dynamic marketer like her to bring in business, she saw, in a moment of clarity, that they were stuck and would be for a long time.

"I'm someone who talks out strategies, talks out figures, plays off ideas and my assistant feeds them into the hard drive," Dee said. "I never thought of myself as smart with machines—in fact, they scare me. But as a friend reminded me, the Information Superhighway sent an off ramp to my back door and I'd better get a map! Okay. But do I have to spend the rest of my career worrying if I can compete on a skills level based on technology? Am I obsolete?"

Christopher Nast, an astute vice president at Colgate, Global Sales, brought the simple truth home about Dee and others in her position. He said:

> To survive on the job—any job—you've got to be very good at what you do and not rely on a company "rabbi" to watch over you. Frankly, you'll have to be a lion, not the wily fox. I mean, you've got to make a very positive contribution, keep the fire in your belly, be unwilling to lose, stay committed to doing a real job and don't take no for an answer.

WHAT ABOUT YOU?

My guess is that like Dee, you're educated, smart and you want a career for the long run. You understand how your company operates as it does. The guaranteed weekly salary check suits you. You may have real ambition—you want to lead, to be a "lion" as Chris Nast describes the strong, long-term leader, not a "fox," more a manipulator who's in to take the money, appropriate much of the credit and run. You can honestly say that you fit into today's work environment and take the good with the bad.

So you may be stable, but the business world is turning upside down and you're not as good at calling the shots. Once, you could deal with a few lay-offs and cut backs in your company. You understood the reason for a merger or acquisition or why a division was dropped or the company folded.

Enough of a fighter to take a stand, you're not a rebel. Neither are you a revolutionary who agitates for change, but you can adapt to it when it presents itself. But then there's now: it's change, revolution, sudden shifts, uncertainty. In fact, it's beginning to look a lot like upheaval barreling down the aisles toward you. Now you're confused, troubled, insecure about what's happening to you and to the people around you. Sometimes you're not sure what your job involves and where you'll be next.

Unlike Edie Weiner, a futurist and management consultant who does not see a "gloom and doom" long-range economic picture, you do! You're wounded and right now you're not quite as optimistic about the future as you want to be. Suppose you landed on your feet when your company last exploded with economic changes, but the earth beneath your soles feels suspiciously unsteady. How long will I keep this job? The question seems to roll around on a perpetual loop. Will I be here for the long term or have to move? You ask yourself again and again.

All in all, perhaps like Dee Archer, you seek the old days when the company was a "fattened calf" and career growth was based on slightly different values. These nostalgic years were when you left work sure your job and the company would be there forever in pretty much the same shape: Fat. If you worked for a large corporation or one supplying the "fat cats," you felt secure! Now multi-national corporations down to small enterprises have trimmed back to fighting shape: the lean machine.

Where does that leave you? Is there enough growth in your company to keep you employed?

If you have no answer, you're not alone. Millions of other people are asking themselves the same complicated questions. Figuring out the state of work in the mid-1990s and your place in it is a heady—but you'll find in these pages—a solvable endeavor.

It's a difficult time for the company survivor. I know you're searching for a reasonable and acceptable explanation for what's happening at work, or, failing that, comfort about a situation you seem unable to improve. Sometimes, the right words don't come. What you do know is this:

➤ **Work life will never be the same**...but that's okay because it can be better! You can find more control and success by learning to take better charge of your career, first of all, by understanding the marketplace. If you accept the fact that corporations and their suppliers will never be the fabled sanctuaries they once were and go from there, you can manage anything.

➤ **Your organization is pointed on a track you haven't been given all the directions to and you feel left out.** But the good news is that there is as much promise in the market as there is polarization—the Labor Department reports that high-wage occupations are growing, creating more opportunities for people with skills, education—and some old-fashioned adaptability.

➤ **Your idea of work and working has shifted from a focus on what the company can do for you to what you can do for yourself.** *Business Week* described a growing phenomenon in companies across America, called "the new contingent worker."

Career builders or people merely interested in staying employed at a satisfactory level may find themselves at a company that's pushing its employers into the organizational fringes. This means you may find yourself making a new kind of contract with the company, large or small, as a consultant, an "outsourcer," a part-timer—or you may even become an entrepreneur.

➤ **Most of all, you'll never go back to business as usual.**

Knowing this, what kind of practical decision can you make about your future? Should you jump ship, stay on or look elsewhere? Most of all, what do you need to know to survive and thrive in the "new" work world?

What will it take now to succeed and guarantee your own lifetime employability?

In 1991, nearly one out of three American workers had been with their employer for less than a year, and almost two out of three for less than five years.

PRICE PRITCHETT AND RON POUND,
The Employee Handbook for Organizational Change

HOW WE GOT FROM THERE TO HERE

So, you're the new breed—the people who have moved out of the industrial age into the techno-information age. It was a shockingly short trip for the amount of change and influence it has wrought. It was a trip charged with wonder, and a real test of human mettle, know-how, intellectual, economic and emotional challenge.

How and why you got to this point in the chain of events started when business structure, theories, practices and technology shifted after World War II. It's a complicated study, but this overview will give you a crash course in sorting it out.

What our fathers and grandfathers understood about work and their relationship to where and how they worked was based on a simple precept: the company you worked for would take care of you. The bigger that company was, they thought, the more secure they'd be. The more upright they were, said our fathers and grandfathers, the more the good life was guaranteed.

Almost every American bought into the dream.

Out of this scrubbed view of the American businessman, was built industry and with it, personal prosperity. Over the years, as the legitimacy of the system was constantly being put to the test, the famous "Organization Man" was given a few shocks to his system, and his complacency.

What happened? I'll backtrack a minute:

The post-World War II boom spawned one of America's greatest age of expansion—forty years of astonishing growth and change. During the 1950s, industry thrived and major corporations, like General Motors and U.S. Steel grew powerful. The corporate focus was on expansion. Companies "diversified," bringing in other products and services, growing into even bigger corporations—the conglomerates, suppliers and professionals servicing these conglomerates expanded to fit the needs. Fat was looking pretty good.

The 1950s was an exciting decade in business—a decade of invention and enterprise. The dubious blessing was born around now— the first credit card—sired by Diner's Club. Remington Rand introduced the world to the amazing Univac 1, the first commercial electronic computer that was room size. At first it was a metal monster understood by very few, and it would be another twenty years before the computer created a huge new industry, new jobs, new skills, new millionaires.

A milestone marked these post-War years, probably one of the greatest changes to implement the democratic ideal: the accessibility of education to any American. America sought literacy, self-improvement. It was a benefit of the new Fatness. Education for every American was a noble experiment that worked so well that it created extraordinary problems. One result was that schools began turning out large numbers of people with advanced degrees. This meant that business had to find an appropriate spot for them. And they did.

As William H. Whyte opined in his book, *The Organization Man,* if the corporation is big, it is therefore good, insuring you success without tears. The brightest, then, gravitated toward the biggest companies, often rejecting better offers from the smaller ones, trusting in size to guarantee security and opportunities for advancement. Big was where the business school graduates wanted to be. Big was most of where you felt you had a future that really mattered.

American businesses in the 1950s were getting chunkier through the middle with deeper layers of middle and upper management. These were "the Eisenhower years," and organization men settled in comfortably with fairly secure jobs and a sense of well-being.

This general prosperity began tapering off as, for one, the political culture of the early 1960s changed what many of us thought about business. While the 1980s were fraught with insider trading and junk bond scandals, the 1960s suffered from price-fixing, bid rigging and colossal frauds and swindles. The more politically liberal environment made it acceptable to probe and expose business practices—and the 1960s statement, "beating the system" meant a way of life to a lot of people.

In the spirit of the vivid '60s expressiveness, many alternate culture radicals, anti-war protesters, health gurus and well-intentioned social scientists took on "big business," de-mythologizing it and opening it up for question. As one total Organization Man told me about the middle 1960s as his career was spiraling upward:

> The Vietnam War years really reshaped attitudes about
> business, and I think, affected the quality of life.
> I was on the cusp of a generation where the whole fabric
> of society began to unravel a bit. At work you felt less like

saying, these people are a part of your family, this place is a part of where you belonged. The attitude loosened the strong ties one had at work.

Before the '60s, you had a measure of comfort and a certain philosophy that helped you succeed within a range. Suddenly there was no more comfortability.

Business never looked so unattractive to so many; "comfortability" was as frayed as Archie Bunker's armchair. The working world was no longer, across the board, a sanctified spot where you were guaranteed security; nor was big tantamount to "good" or privileged; nor could you count on the an inevitable marriage, based on loyalty, between employer and employee, 'til death do they part. Instead, the corporation took some punches—with product safety and planned obsolescence, for example, under scrutiny.

Then in the 1970s, inflation was the story that never went away. OPEC gained power in the global oil business while America's oil business sputtered along. Then the mighty conglomerates got into trouble. In the late 1970s, there was a lot of takeover and merger activity between companies, a precursor of what would mushroom in the next decade. But now, takeovers were likely to be perceived by organization man more as "a smart company taking over a poorly managed one with a good product" rather than seeing it as a move to expand, diversify or as an early sign of greed.

The 1970s did have something to say for it: business was making a real effort to inject energy and intelligence in the slightly anemic corporate system. It created new middle ranks to accommodate college and "B-school" graduates, but companies overextended themselves and created too many jobs. We chugged along with this great economic engine, fueled by a surfeit of middle and senior managers, companies still generating enormous wealth and opportunity.

The Reagan years, in the 1980s, brought with them an economic maelstrom—the decade known for debacles and growth. A lot of business flew apart and altered the shape of the business world as we know it. There was the control of inflation, the collapse of OPEC; savings and loan catastrophes were widespread and "debt bombs" of loans not repaid exploded around us. Organization man, for the first time in forty years, began to feel unsure about his place in the corporation.

Frank Stone*, an engineering technician with a top telecommunications company, told me a not uncommon story of the near religious conviction in the power of "bigness." He bought into the "security/be-a-cog-and-give-into-the-group" ideology in his twenties, choosing to work for a company he believed would never be caught in union squabbles or ever be dismantled, waver or betray its employees—the phone company.

He said:

> My parents worked at a large manufacturing company and both of them lost their jobs or struggled to stay afloat because of union problems. Their worry about security shaped my choices. I always looked for the source of real security.
>
> I didn't want to work in a factory and I didn't trust that a small business would grow so I could grow old with it. So I chose the phone company. I worked for them 150 percent for over twenty years. Management changed. There were new pressures. We were like puppets, our strings being pulled somewhere up from corporate headquarters.
>
> Then the split came. I was out of a job.
>
> Where are the old days? Who can I trust? I'm 55 years old and out of work—phased out after giving them my life.

The 1980s held a surprise for him.

To his horror, "Ma Bell" ripped Frank and thousands of other believers like him from her bosom with the birth of "Baby Bells," a shock Frank is still trying to quell. His anguish is echoed across the country. As a carrier of the torch of the rightness of Organization Man toward the organization, he feels betrayed.

While such cataclysmic changeovers were taking place, so was there growth and innovation, especially in computer technology. Computers literally transformed business—and made from itself a new industry—and new millionaires and billionaires like Microsoft's William Gates. By doing so, computers reached out to revolutionize other businesses, streamlining some, reinventing others, allowing astonishing speed and innovation at a touch of a key.

The inevitable globalization of business begun in the 1970s gained momentum now. America took a few mean blows in the gut. We staggered under an avalanche of imports, especially from Japan, which gained world power status in trade, capturing 20 percent of the market. American corporations began to examine how to come back from the dead. They were losing customers as Japan built factories, bought real estate and invested in America.

The 1980s, will be remembered mostly as the age of takeovers and junk bond scandals and leveraged buyouts. Avarice and some baroque tales of rascality destroyed careers—many of which belonged to innocent bystanders, like you—and wrecked companies. Basically, these were greed-motivated deals that were fundamentally unsound.

Engulfed by debt and foreign competition, corporations could no longer afford the luxury of our legacy—people like you—the educated, middle and upper ranks of organization man and woman. Business is trying to clean up from its disasters—savings and loan crises, leveraged buyouts, bad debts, oil spills—and trying to redesign itself.

The 1990s opened trimmed to the bone. Companies across the board—for profit, not-for-profit, from the Fortune 2500's to the neighborhood grocery stores—determinedly on the lean lane, continue to issue cutbacks or put freezes into affect.

Signs of the Times #1:

We're living in a radically-changing job market—and where are the jobs? The **fastest growing** industries according to *Standard & Poor's Compustat* are:

forest products	machine and hand tools
gas utilities	
cars and trucks	auto parts and equipment
savings and loan	
railroads	computer software and services
publishing	
miscellaneous services	apparel
miscellaneous leisure	beverages
building materials	transportation services

The biggest truth, for which we are all due a bunch of roses for shining through, is that the 1980s fed us a dose of reality about work life. Some of it thorny. We were loyal! We worked hard! In the real world of business, painful things have to be done or have to be faced. Not only is there possible loss—downsizing, cutbacks and bankruptcies—but a reassessment of what work can offer you. You are left asking yourself, who am I in the scheme of things?

Diane Moore*, a dynamic 34-year-old woman in the high-growth computer business, is another example of why life is so different now. Her company was sold, and she was asked to stay on. Loving her product and her job, Diane remained in her office, believing she could adapt to any shifts. It was not to be. Her voice resonates for a lot of people in her situation. She said:

> It was a 30-year-old company, with a certain style that died overnight when the new management took over. They were hard edged. No one really looked at product, just the bottom line. No one looked to see that I had taste, or that I knew what I was doing, or how well I knew the market, the niches and handling the inventory. They didn't care how creative I was, but only, "Diana, did you bag another client?" It all revolved around numbers.
>
> It was tough for me to admit that the new management didn't value me. I soon left the company I thought I'd be with another fifteen years and I became a freelancer. A new torture.

Diane believed she was a woman born without the temperamental "x-factor" that happily propels people through the tensions of freelancing or entrepreneurship. These people suffer most without company structure to set the days. But this company crisis and the tone of the late 1980s forced her into another way of thinking.

Although she had specific notions of how work was "supposed to be," her theories weren't valid any longer. Diane took a chance on herself and joined the other 12 million people who embrace a life of self-reliance in business. In fact, in the last decade, Americans pursued a fitting entrepreneurial life with a vengeance. The rate of new businesses being incorporated in 1994 alone hit over three quarters of a million. Add to this legions of freelancers, consultants and career hoppers who all have one thing in common—a daunting array of new skills that have made them more adaptable, independent and tougher-minded than those who proceeded them.

And Diane? After two years "on the street" as a consultant, she got a sweet offer from a client that she couldn't turn down. Her employability bloomed when she was "Diane Moore, Inc." Independence gave her a new confidence, access to new contacts, and exposure to new ideas. Her own business proffered the opportunity to explore other markets and expand her expertise. It paid off in a way that is meaningful to her: the trade-off is "security" with a growing company to calling her own shots.

Signs of the times #2:

The Bureau of Labor Statistics reported that three industries together accounted for 25 millions jobs, or **one-fifth** of the nation's employed—educational services, health services and eating and drinking places.

And then there's the case of Tom McCann. Of the more than two hundred people I interviewed for this book, no one man embodies an inspiring new independence more than he.

If ever a man ardently believed in the *modus operandi* of the corporation and honored the sense of belonging to a big machine it is Tom McCann, a former corporate director at Bristol Meyers. A charismatic personality, a striking 6'5" tall, Tom, though he held a law degree, chose to put it aside and enter the field of corporate communications.

Corporate people chose jobs at companies where they traded off individuality for security. Tom fit the corporate ideal, the way, for example, a Ray Kroc—the founder of McDonald's—fits the ideal entrepreneurial personality. Let Tom tell it:

> I could own the most successful company in the world, McCann and Sons, and employ thirty people but I wouldn't be as happy as I am now being part of an organization. I love being the leader of a team. I enjoy watching other

people succeed. I know the difference between being creative and not being cooperative. I like the sense of long-
term belonging.

But what's wrong with this picture?

Although a successful corporate player, Tom's story of crisis and
"survival" really begins with his last few years at General Foods, where
he worked for over 20 years and reaching the 38th spot from the top.
Tom believed in the company; there was a sense of pride in the product he was selling every day and the way in which the corporation
operated and handled its employees. He felt there existed "an institutional momentum and character" that business reversals couldn't
dent or eliminate.

With General Foods, Tom saw security and longevity since the company, in the 1960s, was considered a good investment—not glamorous
but solid. General Foods was, Tom said, "the great lady with high integrity, high quality and impeccable kitchens who will be there forever."

Tom felt that "comfortability" at General Foods, until the rumors
started flying in the mid-1980s—rumblings about a takeover. Other
rumors said that it was about to happen at Nabisco, too, the largest
food company in America, and so could it happen to General Foods,
which was number two.

The smoke signals were getting more frequent and soon easier for
Tom to read; they were being sent up by Philip Morris—a tobacco company looking for a good buy. Concerned, Tom conferred with his boss,
feeling that as "cash rich" as General Foods was, the company wasn't
taking precautions against a takeover, nor were they buying other companies and expanding. "We felt invincible," Tom said. He was told he
had nothing to worry about. General Foods was not for sale.

His sense of unease persisted as the months rolled by. Again he
inquired and was assured by higher-ups that "they'd never mislead him."
But then in late September of 1985, the number two tobacco company
merged with the number two food company after three days of negotiations—and Tom's perceptions were proved right. General Foods, to
Tom, would never be the same. The rumblings were stronger still that
R.J. Reynolds was still hunting Nabisco, which they eventually captured
in what is still the highest takeover price in history.

Tom felt betrayed about the General Foods takeover and how he'd been pacified and misled. Before the merger, Tom was about to become an officer. Now, he was part of a division. Still functioning as director of communications, Tom, sitting in his glass-enclosed office, fielded calls from the press. He had a fantasy of the building stoned by angry stockholders:

> I thought, what a damn fool I am. I'm going to be found dead here with a shard of glass through my heart telling people how wonderful it is to be taken over.
>
> In truth, I didn't much like what was happening. I just didn't find a community of interest with them. They were smokers. Tougher. A different operating style. They were not the girl I brought to the dance. There was this new girl and I knew I didn't want to continue being around her.
>
> I was dedicated to this company and thought I'd spend the rest of my life there. I felt they'd treated me well. I was proud of the product. That was all gone.

Feeling the company in its new incarnation was wrong for him, Tom knew he couldn't stay. When he got a call from a headhunter about a position at Bristol Meyers, for the first time in 20 years, he considered changing jobs. He soon gave General Foods notice, although leaving "still felt like the loss of a limb." He said:

> I was the first of the top forty executives to leave. They thought I was crazy and told me, "You're highly respected here, how can you go?" Easy! This wasn't the General Foods I'd known for years. I saw around me massive denial of the changes, the bitterness, all of it. But I also know that such behavior is not an unusual reaction to a tragedy.
>
> You may deny that the company's changed, that it can't pursue what it felt was important before—but it has changed. I probably have a higher sense of moral indignation about takeovers and who takes over than other people. My conscience wouldn't let me stay.

At Bristol Meyers, Tom found that it was "as good as you get in the early 1990s." But good as it could get didn't feel like enough. He looked around and saw that there was no such thing as a sure thing anymore.

Unless you own the company—or have a slice of it through a partner-ship—you have very little power to influence the decision to buyouts or mergers. When the rumors began rumbling through the halls of Bristol Meyers, he knew they were dangerous tremors—he'd walked through rubble before. Experience had toughened him.

Tom made another smart move. He began looking for a new oppor-tunity while he was still employed. He evaluated his position. Trusted his gut reaction. Took adaptive action before it got too late. Then, to his great surprise, the man who never wanted to hang out his own shingle hammered in the first nail; now Tom, who had never practiced law, became of counsel in a Massachusetts law firm and is having the time of his life.

What specifically inspired Tom McCann to eventually become his own man? He assessed company cultures and jumped adroitly from one large corporation to another, then in a surprising move, to a small partnership. Thinking like a chess player, he became more of a master as he practiced each move and learned the rules and infinite possibil-ities of the board he was playing on. As players changed, so did the nature of the game: He could decide whether he wanted to play or get into another game.

Out of this experience, Tom believes, as do many of you who've had similar experiences, that you cannot have loyalty to a company forever. Instead, he would advise his children to "have a duty to your company, come from integrity and do the best you can. But don't be blind to any other opportunity. Take it."

WHERE ARE WE GOING NOW?

The kind of work force making up today's business world may not get a boost up the "ladder of success" as a reward for diligence and com-pliance. Instead, there are the realities of the 1990s and beyond to deal with.

The people who make it and thrive are those with good antennas aimed directly at zeroing in on when to stay, when to move internally and when to move on. Those of you who'll succeed will be the most sensitive to what's happening in your company environment and be-come most capable of figuring out how to adapt to change and benefit yourself.

Larry A. Evans, executive vice president and founding partner of Right Associates, an international human resource consulting firm specializing in outplacement and key executive transitions, has an incisive take on awareness, dealing with company change and what it takes to keep your employability edge. He told me:

> A first, second or third downsizing, a merger, or big change starts a panic all sides feel. Employees are beside themselves. Stress and anxiety is high, productivity is low and people start to move toward a "work paralysis." So we've got the people who are left after two or three cuts working—and often overworked—while the senior management knew they were no longer trusted.

Sound familiar? Larry continued:

> Management has their own way of coping with change or crisis—they can deny things are bad and keep their doors closed or become so task-oriented they're myopic to their own feelings and those of overworked or overstressed employees.
>
> Others hold their head up and say, "I'm going to make the best of this change."
>
> With your head up you can evaluate the changes and the system, where the control is and whether or not there's still internal respect. The height of self-defeating behavior during the shock of change is to publicly demean the values and changes going on and call them "dysfunctional" or worse. This is one way of making sure you don't stay in the organization.

What's the true answer? If you're staying, you are least vulnerable if you've done three things.

> ➤ **First, pay attention to the changing market conditions.** Be proactive in helping your company address the changing market so that you're adding value. Understand the company's budget, find out what your department's long-term and short-term goals are, how it can be more effective in terms of either quality or profitability. Figure out what

skill sets you need to assist the company in getting what they want.

➤ **Second, both you and the company should perceive your place and your responsibilities as adding more value than you are getting paid.** To stay, see where the company is going, where the resources are and what the emphasis is. Let people know you are plugged into this future, but don't brag about what you know. Develop the people under you—create a constant flow of talent and resources. Know you are not indispensable. You can make yourself more valuable, but in the modern company requirement, no one is indispensable—everyone has a successor.

➤ **Three, be willing to change**.

FINALLY

The *New York Times* did a fascinating report on Paul Leinberger and Bruce Tucker's book, *The New Individualists*. Leinberger is the son of one of the original executives interviewed in Whyte's *The Organization Man*. Leinberger hoped to discover if there was a "pass the baton" legacy from these fathers—men who prospered in the '50s and '60s in corporations—to their sons and daughters. What would the legacy be? How would they advise their children to choose a company to work for; would one-time Organization Men insist their children be loyal to organizations, or would these fathers suggest that they strike out and be entrepreneurs, consultants or freelancers?

Leinberger showed that as their fathers retire, the 90s worker wants to work differently, with "a new balance in his/her compact with the organization," or they'll leave if they don't get it.

"Less competitive and more cooperative," the new version of the worker is pouring "more psychic energy into family and community."

What I found to be true among the hundreds of people I spoke to is that, in place of unquestioning loyalty, there is devotion to work itself or to a profession and the right to seek fulfillment in how we spend eight or more hours in the work place.

So let's start here and look at what you need to know to stay in, and stay in at your best.

WRAP-UP

➤ There are two commodities you must have in the work place of the 1990s and into the 21st century—a continuing attitude of adaptability to change and updated technical skills.

➤ You must be good at what you do and be a lion, not a wily fox.

➤ The company you work for is probably in some state of change. Organizations will never again be the fabled sanctuaries of employee loyalty and job security they once were.

➤ Change in the work place has gone from the industrial age into the Information Age and you may not be sure what your job involves and where you may be next.

➤ Millions of people are trying to figure out where to go from here for job satisfaction.

➤ Be aware of the changes in a trimmed-to-the-bone company—which is typical of how most companies are behaving economically as we move into the 21st century.

2

CORPORATE CULTURE:
KEEPING YOUR FINGER ON THE PULSE
OF THE COMPANY YOU WORK FOR

There's a colorful tale that comes from a pioneer in market research, a professor at Columbia University. His assignment for the A&P was to research why people buy what they do, and what their behavior is like in the supermarket. One day he interviewed a woman at the soup display, asking her, "Which one will you buy?"

She answered brightly and without a moment's hesitation: "The chicken noodle...and the tomato." His next question was to find out why she chose those in particular. She answered, "They're the only two flavors my family likes."

The researcher continued, "Well, there are all these other brands and other varieties of soup, why don't you try them?" Again she said, "My family won't eat them. They'll only eat chicken noodle or tomato." He said, "What brand are you buying?" She said, "Campbell's." He said, "There are other brands here. Why did you choose Campbell's?" She said, "Obviously because Campbell's has such variety!"

Interesting story. Our shopper didn't want any soups other than the two she always bought, but she chose the brand because they had over 30 varieties of soup mixes she'd never sample. She wanted the right to choose or reject them.

The story struck me because it reminded me of why so many of us are not only struggling with the meaning of work, but have to figure out what the work place means to tell you about itself. The stuff it's made of. Like our passionate shopper, we're loyal to a few flavors and don't have a taste for the others. We may feel stuck—empowered only to "buy" or buy into a limit of some sort.

The work world comes in thousands and thousands of varieties—"name brands," so to speak, not unlike Campbell's. There are the mixed bags, like the cigarette companies which own breweries; insurance companies that own airlines and snack food factories; entertainment conglomerates owned by Japanese electronic giants or utility companies which are regulated by government agencies, and so on. Each company can be said to have a style, based on certain ingredients that make it, uniquely, for example, Campbell's or Nucor Steel or Liz Claiborne or Paramount Pictures.

These ingredients are not just the products that come off its lines, but the goals, the esprit de corps, the size of the company and how it's managed, the myths it perpetuates, the location, the corporate vision, the logo it creates, the temperament, from the CEO on down. Translated to the business world, these ingredients make up the heart of a company or its corporate culture.

How and what we're told will be expected of us—like our job responsibilities and deportment—is one slice of the corporate culture pie; but the "vibes," the attitudes, the delicate balance between people is not as easily put into words. Most of us are intuitively aware of a company's culture. We understand it or agree with it totally—or just enough—to fit in.

Tom McCann, who was introduced in the previous chapter, is the paradigm of a man who amply documents the power of corporate culture and its relation to employee productivity and loyalty—that is, until he was ready to become his own employer. But look at his history: For over 20 years, Tom believed in General Foods, its values, its products and the expectations it had of its employees. When GF was taken over by Philip Morris, the smoke rose from the new fired-up corporate culture and he felt, though it wasn't true, that his career there was in ashes. Unable to connect with the incoming persona and products, he chose instead to leave because of the culture, not on account of his position or his responsibility to work itself.

Deborah Nash, an attractive, high-energy Californian in her early-30s was formerly a marketing executive at the Disney corporation, is another fine example of flexibility of fit in very different cultures. She began her career at Clorox in northern California, then moved to Disney, in Los Angeles, and then back north to join Yes Entertainment, then a start-up operation. I asked her to describe the experience of maintaining her employability in such contrasting cultures. She said:

> I thought I fit in at Clorox, but to my surprise, the head of marketing at Clorox told me when I left for Disney, "You know, you're really a good intuitive marketer and that just doesn't go over well here." Thank you very much! I think she meant that the analytical side is what mattered at Clorox, not as a back-handed compliment.
>
> Disney, I've got to say though, is definitely made up of intuitive marketers. At Disney, there doesn't have to be a lot of analysis. If anything, it's all gut judgment and sometimes a battle of judgments.
>
> But to compare the companies? At Clorox, the pace could be four steps forward and three steps back, but the four steps could happen very frequently. The same could be said for Disney. They might say, we're doing these four things then reverse the decision and go backwards. So you'd have to be willing to live with that kind of craziness.
>
> Now at Yes, you have to have a strong stomach for budget cuts or sudden management shake-ups and not get into too many conversations about "can the company make it."

While Disney was not quite an ideal culture to her, the job was a wonderful learning experience for Deborah, in a way, preparing her for Yes Entertainment. She said:

> I'm more confident about trusting my intuition. Before, I might have overanalyzed an idea, put it forward and let myself be talked out of it by someone else. The culture here allows me to be productive. It's my priority. I think the key that makes people employable both in their own

minds and in the minds of the company is that you can produce results and stay clear on what results will make a difference.

Tom and Deborah are tough and adaptable, each in his or her own way. We're all complex creatures of habit, and, to backtrack a minute, let me answer the question: How is dealing with corporate culture like choosing or rejecting soup?

Some of us are loyal to a few flavors and hesitant to taste others. The problem is we're confident that we won't like the experience and/or worry that it won't like us. We may feel frustrated, stuck, bored or even defensively short-sighted believing there is only one "recipe" for us and there may be danger in exploring others.

Food and work are never more subject to the same consideration than when you apply the idea of taste and temperament. We all know the person who'd prefer the insecurity of a freelance life or manual labor than work in an office, especially for the government. His or her reasons: for this person, office culture is too predominating a bureaucratic entity, with too many rules, too much red tape. Even the higher odds for job security are not motivation enough to take any 9-to-5 position.

Or, alternately, you may consistently be able to find the right job for the time and thrive in a culture that provides what you need. Professor Boris Yavitz, a Paul Garrit Professor of Public Policy and Business and former dean of the Columbia University Graduate School of Business, pointed out to me:

> What's most important to understand is that managing business is as much or more about managing people and spirit as it is managing things and numbers. An organization functions not on paper but by flesh and blood.

The key to understanding how the company works and identifying the circumstances that create productive or stressful working conditions for you. A closer examination of corporate culture and how it works should help you figure out what you need to thrive in the company you're in or show you it's time to move on.

> "I don't want any yes-men around me. I want everybody to
> tell me the truth, even if it costs them their job."
>
> SAMUEL GOLDWYN,
> *legendary film studio head*

FIGURING OUT THE LAY OF THE LAND

You know the common sense definition of corporate culture, because
you probably hear yourself say things like:

➤ "That's the way we do things here. Don't ask why."

➤ "This gizmo is what the XYZ Company stands for..."

➤ "If you want to make it here, you'd better join in and be
part of the family."

➤ "This place is run with a sweatshop mentality. They may as
well hang a sign in your office that says, 'Be grateful for
your job.' "

➤ "They want workhorses pumping out a 90-hour week. Here
it's produce or die."

In itself, corporate culture is neither good nor bad until it's measured by those it affects—you. It can be the details you learn about a
company at any time along the path to employment—before you even
have your first interview. (It's a good old-boy network. No need to apply unless you've got the genealogy.) Or, it's what you instinctively pick
up at your desk that helps you get along or get what you want. (Follow
protocol to the letter. The person you bypass can have your head.)

So while culture is company etiquette, so to speak, so is it a stronghold of order. Culture can provide a sense of stability, perpetuate certainty in tomorrow, solidify order and create meaning in your life, in
profound ways. At its best, culture is an effective collaboration between
every tier of management and labor, suffused with a specific spirit set
in motion from the top down.

DuPont CEO Edgar Woolard said that, "employees have been un-
derestimated. You have to start with the premise that people at all levels want to contribute and make the business a success." *Fortune*
magazine concurred, saying there's a "basic lesson" that "sounds like a

Confucian principle: Cultural change must come from the bottom, and the CEO must guide it."

By virtue of who he is, the CEO will automatically set the tone...and create a culture. This appears never to be truer than in the case George Haggerty, an expert in franchising companies, who tells the story of a culture that is set by a driving personality, smart management and profitability. The company is Hair Club For Men, and the founder and CEO is Sy Sperling. George, who worked with Sperling to franchise the Club, told me:

> Sy is a fountain of ideas, some of them great, some fair, some not worth worrying about—but he needs people to listen to them. That's how he worked out his plans. He'd drop by my office or phone in and try ideas out. He'd debate with me and others and take criticism. Mostly, he loved leadership, was brilliant at it and knew a lot more about his particular business of hair replacement than anyone else.
>
> You have to be willing to listen to work with Sy. He'd listen to you only if you got on his wavelength and understood his motivation.
>
> Mostly, he was passionate about what he believed in and passionate about helping other people. His attitude permeated the whole organization as well as the consumer field. He is probably one of the most recognized personalities in American business because of his TV exposure. He often laughs about his nasal New York twang, but people love his approach—and his genuine passion shines through.

What about cultures that are not quite so leadership driven? Fragmented or embattled cultures are hard to change and ingrained cultures, especially ones with long ancestries, are nearly impossible to budge ("We've always done it this way," is one catch phrase.) "When events rupture meaning, people will do almost anything to recapture the status quo, to restore their existential pillars," says authors R. Kilman, M. Saxton and R. Serpa in their book, *Gaining Control of the Corporate Cultures*. Moving on means we've got to let go and deal with the uncertainty of transition.

Restructuring and organization—after a merger or downsizing, for example—can shoehorn in new cultures or drop them like a bomb on everyone involved, leaving emotional or professional casualties in the rubble. I asked Professor Yavitz what change does to a culture. He told me:

> I think if you ask middle managers how their company is being restructured—that is, how did management handle cutting people off and how did they treat the ones who remain—you'd get a profound answer. You can tell by the tone of the voice, and the substance, what the real culture is—what the real feeling is. You'd know what would happen if the sword is being waved and you got in the way. If you got cut, would anyone say good-bye or not?

Let's take a look, then, at the anatomy of a culture—the tones of voice, the structure, the brandished swords, the feelings as they may relate to your situation:

INSIDE CORPORATE CULTURE

In their book *Gaining Control of the Corporate Cultures,* author R. Kilman et al., noted that organizations are "rational instruments created primarily to accomplish goals." When we become employees, "ostensibly immune to deeper emotions" at the office, something happens. How right they are.

What most of us are not immune to is an unconscious emotional connection to the company that tells us, this office, this building, this department, these people we work with are family. And it's family with all the attendant human responses—love, loss, grief, "sibling rivalry" via competition with colleagues, envy, anger, loyalty and divided loyalties, favoritism, a sense of pitching in to keep the family together, functioning and healthy.

Some companies play parent to the hilt, infantilizing employees to remind them who's boss. Others attempt some sort of hearty democracy, where employers become pals with employees—sometimes ending when an overconfident employee oversteps a boundary with an employer and puts his job in jeopardy.

WHAT IS THE FAMILY CONNECTION ABOUT?

A corporate environment can easily be set up to feel like a parent-child relationship, sustaining, nourishing, controlling or punishing us. In *Corporate Cultures* by T. Deal and A. Kennedy, the authors noted that successful companies are those that give more "attaboys" (and "attagirls") to their employees than those that don't. A nice pat on the back. Even chairmen, not immune by virtue of their lofty position, look for attaboys from their board of directors.

There's always someone to turn into an unconscious parent-substitute at work, to make us feel appreciated. And not only through attaboys—there are other signs that tell us we're special: nameplates on the door, a windowed office or an office with a second window, a higher floor, better title, huge end-of-year bonuses, the CEO's confidence and ear.

The fear factor ("better not, boy," or "better not, girl") is another common tough parent company style, a holdover from millennia of commanding officials (whether they are pharaohs, feudal lords, land-lords, tax collectors, bureaucrats or sharks) holding the reins over those who have less, or who labor. Fear as a guiding principle, however, in-fantilizes a culture in any era.

I spoke about the culture of tyranny with Joanne Ragovia, a psycho-analyst who was formerly vice president of Human Resource Development, Organization and Staffing at Kidder, Peabody in New York. The people most affected by it, Joanne thinks, are those who carry with them a "womb to tomb" work ethic. She said:

> The child in us needs a home and we look for love in all the wrong places—at work. We want a sense of acceptance and connection, but the culture is about keeping people fear-ful. Instead of being valued, the company keeps their ap-proval conditional. You have to perform or get the right "godfather" or "rabbi" or be a smart political animal.

The "fear" culture is always at high tide—there's a constant testing of waters, or else you feel you might drown. Caught in such waves, you look for little signs of approval and disapproval with each word and every act and watch upper management every day to see if you're in their good graces or not. Rule-by-fear squelches creativity and team work based on trust. Career becomes a burden of chores with one goal, a paycheck. Joanne added:

> The consequence of a fearful culture is also loss of integrity. You figure out what they want instead of what you believe is right—your every act is to guarantee survival. So you cover your behind, you don't take risks, your antenna is always out to see which way the wind is blowing. Are you stuck there? You need to reassess whether this is the right place for you, is this work satisfying or decide, I'm going to stay but I'm not going to let it drive me crazy.

I spoke to two extraordinary women, each of whom worked for large corporations whose cultures bore immediate comparison—the cut-'em-off-at-the-knees forbidding father—the high-octane fear factor—and the cool, but equitable uncle. Cynthia Sonsteile, an executive in industrial relations for Simpson Timber in Washington state thrived in a culture that was generally fair-minded; Helen*, a former utilities consultant and senior vice president for Corporate Relations with Shearson Lehman in New York. There, she focused on public utilities for 40 companies in the U.S., and toughed it out with this competitive culture's effect on the people who keep the machine going.

Helen told me:

> Lehman Brothers was very unhappy, a rigid, patriarchal, non-productive bureaucracy. The financial work attracted entrepreneurial types, but an entrepreneurial culture could not thrive there. I was there almost nine years, and in my last year, there was a dramatic transformation.

The transformation Helen speaks of made news. For one, Shearson Lehman lost one billion dollars in 1990. But in the early and mid-1980s, you could double your salary on Wall Street, "when life was good." Before things started toppling and Shearson Lehman fired hundreds of employees, the culture was high pressure. It went with the territory and the industry. Helen explained:

> There was a formula for each class of employee, a link between performance with incentive compensation. I had a

friend who was tearing out what little hair he had left because he'd gotten one percent less than a colleague, and he felt unsuccessful and unappreciated!

This was a guy who moved the firm from a merit system to a "lock step" program. This was "it doesn't matter what you do or what department you're in. If you were with the company X number of years, and the company made Y profit, you got Z bonus. That was the lock step."

You may work for a company still wedded to this style. However, some say that a smattering of law firms are the last real bastion of collegiality and compensation systems which blur the measure of performance, the number of years with a firm and how much business you generate for them. It was lock step, though, that put Shearson Lehman up there with them. As Helen said, ironically, about this aspect of making money on Wall Street:

> It was one-for-all, all-for-one and if you started linking it to other things, it destroyed the social fabric. It was like socialism, but on a smaller scale.

When the company hit the cold, gray wall, everyone was unsure of his/her job. Keeping with the culture, Helen found that she was not getting the information she needed where the company was going or any assurance that she was safe. She wound up demanding an answer from the man to whom she reported, following him into the men's room when he tried to sandbag her!

Cynthia Sonstiele, working at a Northwest timber company, saw changes come at Simpson which were tough on a lot of people. The company shifted from producing timber to doubling its output of paper over the last 20 years, but it was geared down a lean track, shutting down some mills. Cynthia told me:

> The most productive managers were innovative and hard working, but when the cutbacks came, if a division was cut, it was cut. You went, no matter what. My department was cut 50 percent in 1981. When we looked at job eliminations, we had to be very sensitive that we weren't discriminating—letting go everyone who was old or a minority or a woman.

Sometimes, it was a crap shoot.

Amazingly, my boss stood up for his department, not wanting another body out and said, "Take me, not him," and they did! He took a stand and they shot him down. He'd been there 30 years and was devastated, and he left angry. But, eventually, it turned out to be the best thing for him.

Helen, a veteran of Wall Street culture and its not infrequent bloodletting tactics, was astonished by Cynthia's story. She told me how her experience on Wall Street compared to this altruistic, if not paternal, gesture:

I'm struck by a guy who'd give up his job for someone else. That attitude is history. If anyone took a stand on Wall Street, it wasn't a stand for someone else, it came from a "one-for-all, all-for-me" philosophy.

At Shearson Lehman, the place was highly-politicized and it didn't really matter what you did or who your rabbi was or how fond of you they were. There always seemed to be an arbitrary or slightly schizophrenic leadership that didn't make sense, at least not to me.

What an interesting contrast in cultures. For Helen, managerial emphasis was on *control*. Such a culture discourages events that become too messy and emotional—her needing to track a higher-up into the bathroom, demanding an answer she deserved to get in a more dignified manner, that is, face to face, without pursuit. Among the operative attitudes of a controlling organization are:

➤ Get the job done.

➤ Accept what I tell you and we'll talk about it later, when I decide there is a later.

Cynthia's company runs more on a culture of constructive dissent. A lucky break. The company operates not only with an eye to profit and expansion, but it tries to be considerate of its employees, which it apparently does much of the time. Timber/paper is also an industry that could not transfer easily to many other locations, the way a stock brokerage could. Partially because it is a local, historically long-lived employer, the company exists not as a lofty provider of income, distinct from the community, but part of the whole, on a more human scale.

Wall Street, of course, is about making money—it's the obvious and undeniable product. Money, and how the company feels about it, is as much a part of the culture as the rites it sets up for "power dressing" or a hard-nosed, non-apologetic demand for long hours. But such a focus on lucre is ubiquitous. Wall Street firms alone are not guilty of such single-mindedness. Alfred Sloan, regarded as one of the great corporate leaders and former president of General Motors—his tenure ran during the 1930s–1940s—said of his success in helping to build the company that "here we don't make automobiles, we make money."

It's a bottom-line approach that makes sense, on one hand, but on the other, it overlooks the process and dignity of work, puts the goals of the corporation at profit-making at any cost and, if it's reckless, overlooks the consequences. It's a philosophy that got out of control in the 1980s. It was called the Greed Decade.

Do companies foster such ideologies, encouraging them in employees or do employees already come armed with visions of the "big score?" Professor Boris Yavitz points, in part, to the business schools for creating the money-first men. In describing to me his two biggest criticisms about business schools, he said, reflecting the same view of Alfred Sloan's remark that...

> They're teaching people to make money, not to make automobiles or shoes or candy, and two, they're teaching students to be short-term oriented—not caring about the future. The attitude is, take the money and run.
>
> Parenthetically, they sure as hell don't teach them very much about ethics or morality. In fact, they're being taught a very self-contained and self-satisfied attitudes, where they only care about themselves not their companies. At best, they'll care about the department they work in the company, not the rest of the world.

Helen saw a lot of this behavior on Wall Street and cited another example of a culture gone mad:

> A few months after I left, I ran into a woman I knew on the trading floor who told me a story that sounded like the reign of terror in the French Revolution.

People were brought into offices and told, "Congratulations, you're now head of this or that department and you've replaced the guy you once reported to." The next day, you're settling into your new office and they call you in and say, "We made a mistake. You're out, too."

Cynthia, still at the timber company, is again struck by the cultural differences. I asked her to sum up Simpson's philosophy and she said:

They're very apolitical and live by "our word is our bond." They're not a game-playing organization. They believe in honesty, based on performance. They're fair.

Of course, the Comforting Mom as a company culture also exists. The general effect is like a plate of warm cookies, but there are occasions when the sweetness is deceivingly noxious—professional empty calories. Comforting Moms are likely to take you out to lunch, assure you of your worth and how much they love you rather than give you the raise or promotion you seek. They're easier to work with than the big-gun game-players, but they are still overseers of your career.

Just as a corporate environment can be set up to feel like a controlling or fair-minded parent/child relationship, so are there corporate style "family rituals" as homespun and emotionally-loaded as a Sunday dinner at Grandma's. Most organizations understand these connections and provide rituals and ceremonies to help us celebrate, motivate and commemorate our achievements and our place in the scheme of things.

There are "employee of the week/salesperson of the year" awards. For one, the Mary Kay company orchestrates elaborate testimonial services with a crowning of a "queen" or induction into an "inner circle" as well as giving sales achievers diamond-studded pins in the shape of a bee or even a pale pink Cadillac for their endeavors.

There is, of course in most every company large and small across the country, the classic office Christmas party where one can cross, gingerly, certain lines of position and protocol and "flirt up or flirt down." There are bonus incentive programs, company picnics, and if your CEO follows the late Malcolm Forbes school of elegant employee relations, you are remembered in his will by being forgiven any personal debt to the company, if you happened to borrow cash from the its coffers while he was alive.

Or, none of the above. Some companies are Scrooges—cut and dry bottom liners with limited acknowledgement at end of year with cash or stock; others are benevolent but frugal uncles. Yet others are somewhere in between.

> "Some luck lies in not getting what you thought you wanted but getting what you have, which once you have got it you may be smart enough to see is what you would have wanted had you known."
>
> GARRISON KEILLOR,
> *author*

HEROES, SCAPEGOATS AND GOSSIPS: COLORFUL ROLES THAT TINT A CULTURE

Just as there are parent figures, so are there the creatures with forked tongues, eggheads, winged feet or cloven hooves—the heroes and scapegoats of an organization's culture. Expect to find some network of bigger-than-life personalities—the geniuses, the brilliant performers, the founding partner, an athlete, astronaut or superachiever, any of which are brought in and become role models for others.

The culture also has another sort of Information Superhighway—it's living, breathing, has a social security number and may plug into any of a number of circuits. Who are they? They are the archivists who remember the minutia of office life, the gossips (who relay information, true or false, playing both ends against the middle) and the spies, secretly playing any end against any point in between.

These characters may seem superfluous to some of us, but these people all have a purpose, a collective informal task that is to carry on and protect the culture. Finally, when things go wrong, fingers point to the scapegoats, blamed for crises great and small. Targeted and sacrificed, if necessary, scapegoats leave the company in a quick but certifiably bloody termination.

Along with this cast of characters is another persona—the image the company creates through a trademark or logo, a symbol that forms an almost primitive connection to the company. This image helps set a tone for the culture and affects how people relate to the company. The phone company and its bell, Betty Crocker (now simply a big red spoon), Aunt Jemima (updated from the kerchiefed "Mammy" to a drawing of a sweet faced Afro-American woman of a certain age); Pillsbury's Pop N Fresh Doughboy, giggling when tickled, the U.S. Postal Service's Express Mail bald eagle all make up an image of the company, contributing to its culture.

RATING SYSTEMS, WORKING SMART AND WORKING HARD

Honda, which is considered one of the best-managed companies in the world, has built into its culture a rather fair-minded practice of allowing disagreement, questioning and contention among its employees. Differences of opinion are accepted within Honda's culture, valued and considered by management, on one hand, and not seen as a threat to job security by those who make the suggestions, on the other.

In this way, employees, from top management down, evaluate the company, and quite simply, rate it. A strike, for example, is probably the most extreme "rating system" employees can use against a company and affect its policy. The company, though, usually has the leverage, enforcing standards and practices that must be met. These are the company's once/twice/four-times-a-year evaluations, as much a part of the company's culture as any other of its qualities. What are the rating systems like and how do they affect you?

First, from the company's point of view:

There's an interesting, although general "30-60-10 formula" that companies apply to describe and rate employee productivity: it says:

> ➤ 30 percent always work hard
>
> ➤ 60 percent respond to how they're treated and
>
> ➤ 10 percent create problems or do a poor job.

Since the company wants the most and the best of its employees, how does the culture handle these percentages? Is it set up to encourage and maximize the output of the top 90 percent by establishing incentives or standards that acknowledge and motivate them or does the culture concentrate on trying to keep the difficult 10 percent from destroying the business? If so, what's the effect on the middle 60 percent—do they feel neglected or overworked? Does the company tend to lose its top 30 percent, who'd rather work in a more positive, forward-looking culture?

Where are you now?

What if you're in the top 30 percent or the middle 60? Does your company's rating system help spur you to reexamine assumptions, goals and keep you thinking? What kind of effect does "the test" at work have on you? Does it make you feel self-conscious, competitive, motivated? I asked two dynamic Atlanta men, both in their early 40s and both in upper management positions for Fortune 2500 companies how rating systems worked for them.

Steve Nogi was a southern regional personnel/human relations manager for Federal Express—and responsible for about 6,000 people. Doug Turnbull is a senior vice president of corporate management at Equitable Real Estate Investment Management Company, the real estate arm of the giant insurance company.

Doug spoke of a complete cultural change at Equitable that took place over the last few years, most of it, he thought, money-driven. Originally, the culture was structured like "the big life insurance company," which was openly oriented toward profit-making as much as it focused on cautious investing and a conservative operation. The 1980s had its affect on them, too. He told me:

> The mutual companies believed that as long as insurance policies were sold and money brought in, it could be invested and no one had to worry about profits.

Then things changed at Equitable and it moved from an institutional to a bottom-line culture, and with it, came another result. He said:

> Interestingly, they didn't so much as cut personnel as much as work us harder, but pay us better, too. There was tremendous motivation. In the beginning, people worked harder, made more money and those who weren't happy, left. Work often meant a 12-hour day and some weekends.

The phenomenon that came out of this was the one-to-five rating system, based on performance; five is outstanding and one is unsatisfactory. One way people deal with the stress of a new rating system is to personally define it, psychologically defusing its power, while still accepting it as law. Doug explained what happened:

> The very simple definitions of "one-to-five" in your own mind is, *five*, you hung out the moon and the boss lays awake at night in deep sweats, worried that you'd leave. *Four* is, you're good, but if you leave, it'll cause him a problem, but not a disaster. *Three* is, you're replaceable so the boss doesn't care if you leave; *two* is, the boss is saying, "Why are *you* still here?" and *one* is, he's never seen you.

An interesting effect took told—the rating system permeated the culture. In the mid-1980s, there were a lot of people at the middle mark, but as the company changed, so did employee standards for themselves. Pressure came from within the ranks. Doug said:

> We couldn't accept a three rating and those of us with higher ratings openly said so. The person who wasn't good enough could be forced out by colleagues, as opposed to management. "You're not working hard enough, you're not pulling your weight..." they'd say. The mindset was compensation, a way of saying to poorer performers, "I'm here working hard and you're not doing your job."

Interesting inter-reaction: employees not only accepted the system, they enforced it among themselves. Steve Nogi, when at Federal Express, experienced something similar. It started because Equitable Real Estate went on a lean track—and a lean corporation changes culture, prioritizing to be more efficient. The new CEO cut $150 million in costs in the first two months of his tenure and revolutionized the accounting system. Steve said:

> He got rid of a lot of people, and the interesting thing is, you can't tell the difference. The company runs better with a focus on what's more important. Communications are a lot more direct, with no three or four layers in the reviewing process.

Then came the rating system. When it was newly instituted, it wasn't welcome, but it soon became a natural part of the culture. People who weren't measuring up felt it, not only as it was reflected in monetary compensation, but as with Doug at Equitable, in terms of their peers. Steve explained:

> Our rating system went from one-to-seven—seven being the highest paid. Employees were evaluated every six months and there was also a system of "paid-for" performance, based on merit, which worked on a different scale for management and non-management. Mostly, it was instituted to reward the better performers.

COMPANY CULTURE CHECK LIST: WHERE DO YOU STAND?

To best survive in a company, any company, you need to understand it "below the skin"—what really runs it, what are its real expectations and what the culture is really saying. The following questions—and some of the answers I got from people in a wide range of skills—will help you analyze your work place. The descriptions you provide to the questions will clarify how to best fit in to the company you work in now or point out why you should decide to move on, move up, or go out on your own.

As you look at these questions, you might rate your company 1-10, with 10 being the highest. When you answer, also do a bit of analyzing so you are clear about what it's like at work and if it is what you need.

> ➤ Is your company committed and competent? Do they have the ability to train, to improve things? Does their vision itself evolve in a way that makes sense? Does it invite innovation?

> ➤ Can company ideology be explained in a meaningful way? Can the company pinpoint any problem dogging it now—productivity, morale, competitive edge, leadership, where it's going?

> ➤ Are company leaders more likely to be tenacious, able to prioritize; are they devoid of self-pity, rarely bored? Does top management contribute a "good word" as well as put troubles on the table?

➤ Does the company rely on money incentives first (or only) to deal with people and solve its problems?

➤ How does the company talk about itself in terms of the economy? If they've got to tighten their belt to get through rough times, how are they telling you? Do they deal effectively with company morale when there are cutbacks?

➤ How are decisions made? Is top management hyperactive, impulsive or dramatically venturesome, channeling hunches and impressions into action rather than considering facts?

➤ Are they slow to decisions, being overly conservative and reluctant to take risks, poring over figures again and again?

➤ Can they get the facts, weigh the credibility of the players and the products, get a reasonable assessment of the outcome and go for it?

➤ Does the company demonstrate accountability and acknowledge best efforts, that is, are your praised for your contributions and successes and held accountable for your setbacks?

➤ Does the company give you a sense of job importance or do they make you feel disposable, not dispensable? Can you manage upward, that is, how do you spur your boss into action?

➤ Does your company expect you to devote a lot of time to the job, or understand that you want to establish some sort of balance between work and a personal life?

Now add up your yes and no answers. If you have:

➤ 10 or more yeses for all or part of a question: You are at a company that's right for you.

➤ 6 to 8 yeses for all or part of a question: You're getting by at your company. These questions should help you figure out what suits you best

➤ 5 or fewer yeses for all or part of a question: You're probably living with dissatisfaction and should seek another company.

FINALLY

When you feel you're valued by the company, when you know that it's okay to make a mistake and that work is not the sum total of your life, you're likely to give more of your creativity and commitment. Such feelings and actions may not make your job secure, but the humaneness of a culture makes you willing to stick through the tough times, if you have the opportunity.

It's undeniable that social and technological innovations within companies will continue and intensify in the future. Rather than slowing down, the scope and pace of change—and change in the culture—will move faster. When that happens, there will be signs and signals—the triggers that will set you on another path at work.

WRAP-UP

➤ "Corporate culture" describes the company style, the company etiquette, even how it may be described by others outside it—"It's an old-boy network." "It's a tightly run bureaucracy." "It's a do-your-own-thing kind of place as long as you do your thing." Even a company logo, like Pillsbury's Pop N Fresh Doughboy, sends a message as to the general tone of the company.

➤ Culture can provide a sense of stability, perpetuate certainty in tomorrow, create meaning in your life—and be a stronghold of order.

➤ Some companies play parent to the hilt and are "paternal" or "maternal," and emphasize the company as a "family."

➤ Other companies choose the "fear" culture, where there top management plays up ideals of competition between employees; there is always less positive feedback or generous signs of approval from management.

➤ With mergers and downsizing, the culture can change as new owners or partners come in or power shifts.

➤ If the culture is compatible, you'll be willing to stick through the tough times.

3

TRIGGERS:
THE SHOCKS AND SURPRISES THAT SIGNAL CHANGE

I gave a speech in Boise, Idaho, a few years ago, addressing an audience of people, almost all of whom worked for utility companies. My message to them, I thought, was relevant and hopeful. I described the new truths about the state of business now—lean, in flux, but still abounding in opportunities in search of risk takers—and also alerted them to what they might face in the near future.

One eventuality for them was that even a utility company cannot guarantee lifetime employment. I heard a murmur rise and could see my audience's reaction to this statement: disbelief, irritation. I continued.

Change, I said, is simply a fact of business life, and I suggested that they be aware of signs and signals of change and that, in fact, some of them may find themselves in a different job in the near future. But this can work out fine if they are tuned in to change, and the rumblings that lead to it. I concluded on an optimistic note.

Optimism didn't matter then. This audience was very unhappy with me. It wasn't a matter of having to break a few eggs to make an omelet; it's as if I'd crushed the egg of a near extinct species of bird! Voices rose in protest.

They asked me, "What does change and mergers and acquisitions and corporate jockeying for top jobs have to do with us? We're public utility companies! What we produce everyone needs, every day." Or, "Aren't you being a bit of an alarmist?" If "Ma Bell" for one, could change shape and its economic path, so could an Idaho power company.

Learning they would not have a lifelong claim to a piece of the realm stunned these Idaho utility workers. They resisted news of change for a long-ingrained reason: it's inconceivable to them that economic trends or management restructuring could catch up to traditional settings and affect them. People who choose careers with government or utility companies do so, generally, because these are the places known for stability and security. But that's changing too.

A government or utility employee may deny a shake-up is in the air because experience and history are pretty much on the side of ongoing convention. They hear the creaks and rumbling as if a foundation is resettling under a load, not fracturing under the weight. And they ignore the signals.

My message that their world is no longer safely contained within the boundaries of lifetime employment at the company is true for them, in a conservative industry, as it might be for you, in a more competitive and progressive one: change is part of the employment picture. Nothing is certain and no effort guarantees survival. It's an important message, too.

The smart company survivor needs to keep his/her antenna up for the triggers that set off inevitable change. If the situation then calls for it, he/she must figure out how to go with change or go elsewhere, adapting or acquiring skills to guarantee lifelong employability.

"Every adversity carries with it the seed of an equivalent or greater benefit."

NAPOLEON HILL,
The Master Key to Riches

TRIGGERS: TUNING IN

Triggers are signals that tell you change is not only on the way, but unstoppable. They're equally subtle and distinct, predictable and unpredictable, influential and capable of shifting the course of your career. In general, you can expect a trigger or two will enter your life as a trend or an event.

The difference between the two depends on how decisions are made in the corporation and how they are set into action. Take trends. They often start as temporary measures—a corporate policy that revives executive travel, cutting back to stay on the lean lane. The trend is frugality for now.

Or consumer tastes influence the actual manufacturing of a product and its marketing. Over the last ten years, for example, the trend in the food business has been toward low fat/low cal/low salt/low sugar. If you run a fast-food hamburger chain, you make certain adjustments in the menu to "eating healthy" or lose your market share. And if you're in other businesses in flux, like the meat business, advertising, oil or timber, you'll have to make some changes or suffer as did Western Union with the advent of overnight mail and the ubiquitous FAX machine.

Whether a trend comes in through economics or technology or policy, the writing will be on the wall. If you're going to be a survivor in your industry, you'll need to look for where the trends are positive by studying the market. More than just a fad, trends change how people live and think until it becomes mainstream ideology. It's to your advantage to tune in to what's happening around you and not bury your head.

You may find a trend shaking up an industry—it moves piece-by-piece to another state (or country) in pursuit of lower wages until the local industry has shrunken appreciably, as with the garment business in New York.

While a trend allows you to be agile and mobile and prepare for change, the event is so sudden that it kicks you into another realm. Sometimes the trend evolves into an event, as exemplified by the garment center. Stitch by stitch, a salesperson told me, she watched production around her move out of town. She thought that what was happening only affected the workers in the back room, but not her.

"The only person whose life it didn't change too badly was the guy who owned the factory," she said. And I'd be willing to wager that even he may have another plan in mind for his future.

You may not be in a similar situation. How do you know you are? Understand your industry.

An event, though, often occurs without warning. Things aren't so apparent. You may have a notion that things are in flux, but you can't predict or pinpoint what they are: your boss comes in and says, "It's all over...we're closing!" and you're amazed and you stand there saying, "How could this happen?" Or management installs someone who is culturally different from you and there is a strong mismatch. You're fired.

In order to survive in the lean lane, you must be original, adaptable and aware. Triggers, by their nature, jolt you into awareness. Here's what they're like.

Triggers my differ, but they have these three intrinsic qualities in common.

> ➤ The **buzzing**: Rumors or information filtering down from the top or surfacing from the middle, tension in the air— it's a predawn scene as the "trigger" is in its infancy. Somehow, buzzwords dominate the conversation. Everyone seems to be talking about cutbacks, the day's stock quotes, change in temperament in top management, absences. If your culture is histrionic, there may be a wave of panic, threats, back-stabbing.
>
>   You must be astute and as tuned in as you can be, weighing rumors against potential real facts.
>
> ➤ The **shock of awareness**: The gun has gone off in one way or another—the company is undergoing some change and the truth is out in the open. Whether it's a cutback, relocation, merger or some other career-altering change, you're either a survivor or a casualty.
>
>   One way the shock waves come home to you: Your boss goes out to lunch and doesn't return. His secretary packs his desk and you're promoted in.
>
> ➤ The **period of adjustment**: If you've been laid off, you've got to get your life in order, deal with termination packages, outplacement appointments, "golden

parachutes," if that's the case. As a survivor, you'll typically go through a gamut of emotion as co-workers exit, including an erosion of trust in the company, and a sense of anxiety based on the fear that your job may be next to go.

The shake-up helps you evaluate more clearly what you want from the company and your career.

Lifetime employment vs. Lifetime employability: Lifetime employment once meant that the company provided you with a job until retirement. The concept of lifetime employment has now gone the way of the wrist corsage—attractive but quaint.

Lifetime employability means you seek growth, make an ongoing effort to improve your skills and can adapt and synthesize your skills into other positions and industries. No matter what the trigger, you can adapt.

THE BIG EVENT: WHAT'S FAIR, WHAT'S NOT FAIR

A research team at Columbia University's Graduate School of Business led by Professor Joel Brockner measured the effects of layoffs on "survivors' work performance" and loyalty to their employers. Brockner found a few points were universally true among his respondents. Chief among them was that it's crucial how management handles a layoff, one of the most emotionally wrenching of work-related events.

Survivors will identify with the people who've been laid off ("That could have been me..."), often feeling guilty that they've survived the cuts. Others feel that they're benefiting from a co-worker's misfortune ("Bob's out. That means I get his corner office..."). While the fascinating eight-year study was taken from the manager's perspective—meant to help them make more informed decisions about handling layoffs—Professor Brockner also got some insight into what employees think. Most, he concluded, will decide if a layoff is a justified event if they think the company is fair and if it was carried out fairly.

Brockner calls the way in which the layoff was handled, "procedural justice," that is, how dignified and respectful management treats employees when delivering the bad news. This includes how they told people, where they were told, when they were told—was in midweek or a Friday. Professor Brockner explained further:

> I've been in companies where managers get into a "can you top this" war story where they share the outrageous ways in which the news or process was handled. Sometimes employees are given cards that say A or B on them and aren't told what either letter means until the A's are asked to stay put and the B's told to move into the auditorium next door and without advance warning, told they're no longer needed.
>
> Sometimes the people who are about to be laid off are the last to know. They might be driving home and hear on the radio that there's going to be a layoff—the company leaked the information to the media before telling its own employees. This, simply, is crummy treatment.

What, then, is fair when a trigger is about to go off?

Fairness usually varies greatly in definition from one situation to the next. The prospect of sudden unemployment is an emotionally-loaded experience in which someone is bound to be hurt. "Woe to the CEO who doesn't convincingly depict a bright future for the company that has just suffered sweeping human resources casualties," said *Industry Age* about layoffs. "There can be few happy tomorrow's for a manager who excels only at sharing the dark at the end of the tunnel."

Can any words make people feel better about "the dark," the dreaded layoff? Professor Brockner thinks that if employees are given a clear and adequate explanation, it's easier to deal with a crisis. And interestingly, it's not so much the content of what's being said as the manner in which it's presented. Makes sense!

Advance notice communicates dignity and respect: people might think the layoff is fairer because they could be given information about the company they hadn't thought of before. A drastic move makes more sense when management takes time and effort to explain.

The Kamikaze approach defines the idea of "procedural justice," as in the following case...

WHOSE JOB IS IT? THE SHOCK OF THE NEWS

If any individual describes resignation about fair play and humane treatment on the job, it's New Yorker Chris Jones, who early one Monday morning, had a "paper bomb" dropped on his desk. At the time, Chris was managing the deposition summarizing service for a division of H.&R. Block, a mass-market accounting firm. A colleague sat on the edge of his desk and showed him an ad that had appeared in the Sunday *New York Times* employment section that looked too suspiciously close to home. Both men speculated.

The ad called for a business manager and deposition summarizer—which could be his boss's or Chris's exact position and title. Other specifications asked for someone experienced in litigation support, who'd be directly responsible for client-based development, work-flow coordination, recruitment and so forth—or, by the end of the ad, a close description of Chris's job.

He had a sinking feeling. Without his suspecting why, a sixth sense told him that the company was shooting him down. That's my job, he thought. But he took a look at his department, who was in favor, who wasn't, who was producing, who was bluffing and Chris felt sure that he was safe. In fact, now he was feeling better: it couldn't be him, he thought, it must be his immediate boss, Laura*. The description could fit her as well.

Chris told me what happened:

> I thought, it can't be me because I'd know it. Jack,* the national director, was a personal friend and mentor and it seemed illogical that he'd fire me without letting me know face to face. Why put an ad in the paper? I wanted an answer.
>
> I immediately photocopied the ad and faxed it to him in Florida and added a note that said, "I've said nothing and await your input." Jack called back and said, "You're wise to say nothing. I'll tell you about it over the weekend."

What could be more assuring? Jack suggested he was coming to the city five days later, that Chris had nothing to worry about, and that he, Jack, was almost taking Chris into his confidence, suggesting that the target was someone both of them could not mention now. Chris was sure that Laura was out. Chris had been hired first, when Laura was brought in over him. He said:

> I didn't think of it as survival when Laura arrived, but continuation. I'd go on playing the game, staying in this position because I was doing so well. I liked Laura, but the truth is she had more sizzle than follow-through and I thought, well, they finally noticed.

A diplomat, Chris asked the colleague, who pointed out the ad, to be cool and not discuss it. If Laura saw it already, she wasn't showing any indication. Meanwhile, Chris set up appointments for when Jack would be in town the following week—he and Chris were set to see some important clients. Memorial Day weekend was coming up; Jack did not keep his promise to call on Friday, but he did contact Chris that Monday morning—a week after he was shown the ad:

> There was talk of me taking over Laura's job since we were both doing the same work by now and I often took the lead. I thought this call would mean a promotion. When Jack called he was straight with me. "Chris, it's your job," he said. Like that. I was in shock.
>
> I'm stability-oriented and I was moving into what looked like riding the crest of this wave, for years to come. I was enjoying the job, it was new and interesting.
>
> When Jack fired me, I had a physical reaction, like I'd been kicked in the stomach. I felt like the muscles that held up my stomach collapsed.

To be easier on him, the firm gave Chris a month's notice rather than ask him to leave that day. But when a trigger is aimed at you and your hide fuels the thrust, even 30 days are cool comfort, especially when you're a top producer and it feels like it doesn't count to your company.

Was this equitable, logical? Chris had been forewarned from the beginning that the company was "cutthroat." He thought he was attuned to the culture, but through it all, he had no sense that cutbacks were about to erupt and that he'd been fired. What he knew was that Jack was considered "rebellious," a bit too flamboyant for the image of the company, but still respected.

Chris could never have predicted whether being "Jack's person" or not could affect him so drastically.

He worked a little psychology on himself to get through the shock, thinking of what was wrong with the job: It required a lot of cold calling, it was high pressure and demanded that they fill quotas of varying sorts. He'd even gained 40 pounds since he'd been hired. Given the economy, Chris was pulling in business and got acknowledged, but getting caught in a political situation was beyond his control. Then he considered Laura and Jack and the matter of fairness. He told me:

> It was like a Mandarin intrigue—who was saving face, who was really stealing secrets or who was running the show, who was on whose side, who'd get knifed in the back? Most intriguing to me was that apparently Laura and the guy, who showed me the ad, knew I was getting fired, and I didn't. I know you don't tell someone they're about to be canned, so that's okay.
>
> I can't think of being fired as fair or unfair. I think the belief that life is supposed to be fair has created more misery on this planet than any other credo.
>
> Fair is a wonderful concept; there are situations that are fair, times you get people who control whole situations and do so equitably. Most of the time the issue of justice isn't greater than the drive for the paycheck—unless it was clearly out-and-out discrimination against blacks or Hispanics or gays or women. I don't expect people to stick their necks out and threaten their positions.

But in an interesting sidelight, Chris's ex-boss Jack, has gotten his notice and is about to be let go. Jack is playing corporate musical chairs, and he's promised to take Chris to his next job. This appeals to Chris, if it happens. Jack is a pioneer in his area and knows Chris is the "perfect second-in-command" type, and a workhorse.

While he could take the reins, what he does best is go over the agenda of the day and what has to be accomplished, and he does it. He's hitched to a star and he's made peace with that.

But there's another issue here. How much information should Chris have been given and does he, as an employee, have the right to such truth?

Chris learned his job was up for grabs when he read it in the want ads. Interestingly, he first thought he was being sacrificed because the company's target was really his mentor, the man who hired him. He later found out that his branch office was not profitable, and the company was suffering losses and had to cut back. What a difference such information makes to someone who has lost a job he'd been committed to.

Should Chris have been made aware of the problem the company was facing? Most of us would say, yes.

TRUTH TELLING: HOW MUCH SHOULD EMPLOYEES KNOW

Termination may not be easy to take, but there's dignity in knowing your work was acknowledged and that an economic trend determined your fate, not an inaccurate appraisal of your skills. Chris Jones may have felt betrayed or unappreciated at first, but when that trigger went off, he was not shot in the back—as was the worker who told me this following story. Bob* was simply "in the wrong seat at the wrong time." I'll fill in the details for you.

Without warning, the CEO of the Fortune 2500 company Bob worked for was summoned before his board of directors. "You want to keep your job?" the man was asked. The CEO certainly did.

"Then," he was instructed, "cut 20 percent of your work force. Today."

The ultimatum was clear—it was either his job or theirs. The CEO turned on his heel and knew what he'd have to do. He headed back to his office, which was an old, converted loft originally built by a large engineering firm. After sizing up the work space, the CEO called over one of his managers, pointed toward the vast room and directed, with a sweep of his hand, "You see the desks from this column over to that one?" The manager nodded. "Well," said the CEO, "everyone who sits there is now out!"

"What do you mean," the manager asked, shocked. "Some of these people have worked here over 10 years."

"That's not my concern," the CEO said, emphasizing his directive with the chop of his hand. "From this column to there...out!"

Too many people lost their jobs that day.

The general environment in many companies may be "perform or die," but performance—good or bad—made no difference to the survival of these workers. They were fired for no reason other than the unfortunately fateful placement of their desks and an arbitrary sweep of a hand by a fearful leader.

Colleen Loader, a Canadian from British Columbia, also has first-hand knowledge about another version of silence and sandbagging. A dynamic blond, Colleen left a secure job as district sales manager for a book chain to work for Penguin Books, in Toronto. It seemed like the perfect job to her, with a product line she loved and believed in.

Given freedom there and not constrained by constant supervision, Colleen excelled. She saw the future opening up for her. The company, she felt confident, was in good shape—as she put it, "the picture looked good and my numbers were great."

Then rumors started flying that Penguin was in a "shortfall," or preparing for a cutback. The trigger had gone off, but no one paid attention. Colleen remarked, even after the first wave of cuts. She told me:

> The company was in too deep and needed to lose salaries. They laid off the sales division across Canada—about nine people, the longest term being 11 years. The rest of us were told, "Don't worry. That's it." We were also told we'd have to work harder, but that we were safe.
>
> That was okay with me.

The president of the company took Colleen's sales division to dinner at the best restaurant in town, and assured them they all had jobs. It is about now that credibility became a work place casualty. Colleen had a gnawing sense that something was afoot. Within weeks of the dinner, the vice president of the company was sent out to fire her. She left with a severance package, medical insurance and they let her keep the company car. I asked Colleen how she thought events led up to this moment. She said:

> Let's start with the president and that dinner. Either she knew there was a possibility of more layoffs and didn't want to face it then, or they were in such trouble that she wouldn't know what would happen next.

In retrospect, I know there was no way for me to save my job. Absolutely nothing. It wouldn't have mattered if I could have made up the million dollars they needed even if I had put in more hours, worked harder, made greater sales.

Now that I'm out, I'm not cynical, but more aware, more prepared. I gave 150 percent for Penguin. I loved the job, but now the thrill is gone.

Getting fired didn't really shock Colleen. Looking back, she told me, she could see how "naive" she was. While there was no real information filtering down from the top, while executives either would not or could not be straight, there was, however, gossip. Belief in the company and a "gung-ho" enthusiasm for the job kept her in her innocence.

How much should management tell their employees about reversals or potential problems. Enough, Colleen believes, to help you make decisions about your life at the company. *Inc.* magazine posed the key questions to a number of CEO's and got a few interesting answers:

One thought there was an impulse by top management to keep employees in the dark, but that doing so was shortsighted, not helpful. Another said that by doing so was shortsighted, not helpful. Another said that by identifying a problem you don't do something "to employees," but rather, "you endure something with them."

The consensus was that sharing bad news with employees may "heighten trust by increasing awareness of future trouble." With bad times, open communication—truth telling—gives you a point of focus. Silence or sandbagging distorts reality and "credibility becomes the first work place casualty."

The result is that everyone becomes obsessed with the subject of layoffs/cutbacks/shutdowns and too much time is spent on speculation (who's going, who's staying). A natural outgrowth is the spreading of rumors—some true, some fanciful and some destructive.

Information, then, is power. You can decide what course to take. Stay and stick it out. Look around for another job. Prepare for the eventuality of getting laid off.

Colleen sees that she should have gone to a higher-up, pressed for some information, especially after the first wave of firings, and "jumped into action," and look for a job. Luckily, things fell right for Colleen, and she moved right into a major sales representative position, a job she took within a week of leaving Penguin.

Now she's tuned into what's happening at her new company in a dispassionate way, armed with more experience and a resolve not to get caught again.

Been fired? Work place lingo may not let you simply be "canned" any more. Euphemisms for losing your job are varied and descriptive, but still take your breath away:

Laid off, downsized, streamlined or right-sized (they were too big); sabbaticalled (time off, but you may not come back); you're out because the company is resourcing (the resources they had before didn't work, so they're resourcing); restructuring. Don't think of it as being out of work, you're career transitioning. The company's making economic corrections and are doing "RIF" or reduction in force; they are flattening, de-layering; reinventing, impacting, excising; they are moving bottom up instead of top down.

THE BIG EVENT: THE SINKING OF AN INDUSTRY

The accomplished and dynamic blond, Jan Strode loved the glory days of working at Firestone Tires, where she was senior first vice president, the highest ranking woman at the company at that time. It was a job that had come to her. She was giving a speech in Boston for Allstate Insurance—a company she loved—when she attracted the attention of a Firestone executive.

Jan was wooed for three months, until she was told she'd have the chance of a lifetime, representing Firestone and "probably go on television to debate consumer advocate Ralph Nader."

She was 32 years old then and she seized the day.

There was glamour, cachet and privilege attached to the Firestone name and Jan loved it. She was a young, smart woman in a visible job in an industry dominated by men, the company and her success in it helped shape her corporate identity. She said:

The corporate engine would start and I'd get on a plane with, say, the Chairman of the Board and fly to see Lee Iacocca at Chrysler. It was a difficult time then for Firestone, which was having serious problems, needing to recall thousands of tires. It meant something to me.

When she married her husband, a San Diego developer, Jan chose to stay in Cleveland with Firestone, rather than relocate to California. Jan started a commuter marriage. Then, through her husband's contacts, "the old-boy network" in California approached her for a job at a savings and loan bank about to go public.

She'd gone through the interview, not really interested in the job, and made them an offer: "Let me know when you go public." They liked her credentials, especially since she was coming from a Fortune 100 company. Four months later, they met Jan's salary requirements and brought her out to run the marketing, advertising, public relations and community relations divisions.

Then the consequences of the savings and loan debacles eventually moved toward Jan. Many Texas and midwestern banks had already been hit. She thought her bank was immune from collapse until she got a phone call from someone "in the know" who advised her, "Jan, I don't think you want to put that new bathroom in your house just yet." For the first time in her career, a trigger that could change her life and career—in this case, a bank audit—came from outside her control. She wasn't ready to believe the warnings. She told me:

> So let's say that in one year I'm in love with my job. I'm actively selling the fact on Wall Street that my bank could be one of the great regional institutions in America.
>
> Then by the end of the year, I'm seeing the unraveling of our real estate portfolio. I've personally lost one and a half million dollars in stock options and, then it was clear—the bank was sinking.

The severity of the situation hit Jan clearly when a meeting was called at 11:30 one night. Fifteen "heavies"—the CEO, lawyers and senior management—were gathered in a huge conference room with a panoramic view of the Pacific. A beautiful setting for a murder. Jan walked into that room and she sensed that this was the end. Bodies would fall.

Since it was Jan's job to write the press release, the instant obligation was to know how bad the situation was—what could management reveal to the media and share with employees until the whole truth was known? It turned out the accounting firm had been auditing their books for years and were suddenly insisting, that they were not signing off on the numbers. A debate soon opened as to whether or not the bank was still "a going concern."

Jan felt that she was witnessing the last hours of a company she'd been so fully committed to. She described it:

> I never knew how deeply I felt about this until I packed my office. The bank hired what I call, "Bank Exterminators, Inc.", a consulting group called in to help management "streamline" us. That meant the layoffs would start.
>
> I thought they recommended cutbacks that were more akin to desecration than streamlining—too many people were being sacrificed. What was going through my mind is people who'd believed in the bank, in its security, who'd just purchased homes, who had families to support. It was horrible.

Even as the bank's stock tumbled from $24 to 75 cents a share, Jan still believed that her four-year contract would be honored. It would mean she'd have the luxury to figure out what to do next. Meanwhile the bank had two options: one, to be seized by the Federal Government, in which case they were sunk, or two, the bank could go on the block. Within 24 hours, senior management went looking for a suitor.

Once blood has been let, the sharks start circling; often, you don't have the leverage to command salability. As Jan put it, "We were a fire sale." All the bids came in sealed. After 60 days, the news was not encouraging. No one wanted to buy the bank as a whole institution nor buy part of it. Jan said:

> I was sick to my stomach. It's part of being a corporate animal. A lifer like me believes in the security blanket and employment and all the things that go with it. It outweighs my wanting to take a risk. I wound up rearranging the chairs on the Titanic in the S&L business.

> Then I was out and now I'm scared to death. This is the
> first time in my life that I've even had to look for work or
> come up with another version of a job I can do.

Out of her experience, Jan has a philosophy about corporate management and what it owes employees. Clarity of vision comes from the top. She believes that unless a CEO enthusiastically paints the corporation's goals every other month and reminds the senior manager all the way down to the file clerks what the company is about and where they're going, then corporations will live in gray all day long.

When companies function in that gray area—what Jan calls "nebuland," instead of in clear black and white, they dysfunction in spite of themselves. Often, it is up to the public relations person to out in ink what they're about, usually in terms of "we're launching a new product today."

A company has to validate who they are as a company—not only what their goals are but their responsibility to shareholders, the community and employees. For Jan, the real shock of that first ominous meeting was discovering that the bank had lived in nebuland and that, as she said finally, "We had to face the fact that we couldn't put perfume on a skunk and sell it."

FAITH IN THE COMPANY

Like Jan, Leslie Smith went through a great company change when the Affinity Group bought the for-profit National Association of Female Executives (NAFE), where Leslie is an associate director. Unlike Jan, Leslie had happily survived one previous company buy-out that brought her to where she is now. With the sale of NAFE—the second changeover in 10 years—Leslie went through a period of great doubt and concern over who these new people would be and how they would affect her job. She told me:

> A lot of questions ran through my head, the second time
> around. Will the new owners keep me on? Will they care
> about me? Will I want to stay? Most of all, will I respect the
> company?

The trigger started with the news of the purchase, then what the Affinity Group was really like soon became apparent. The first thing they did was distribute to everyone at NAFE an "employment manual," a handbook on what the employees should know about the company moving in. They included every detail—their mission, employee health benefits...down to their policy about smoking. Leslie read through it and felt heartened, if not relieved:

> I thought, this is a company that cares about its employees. The change became less threatening because they were so reassuring. I felt, I want to be included in this partnership.
>
> This was followed up by a yet more reassuring event. They came to our office and sat down with each one of us. Instead of being a phantom management, there was someone to brief us.
>
> It showed they cared about the whole person. They treated us like assets.

Leslie still has a few question marks about the purchase. NAFE is a woman's organization with woman's concerns in business and will some of "the old-boys' network" thinking somehow creep in. "But that's America!" Leslie says, philosophically.

What becomes clear as culture changes to adjust to the new ownership is that there are, inevitably, more layers, more paperwork, more memos. Leslie said:

> I don't mind any of this because all the triggers indicate that Affinity has resources that translate into money and staff and that means growth.
>
> Without sounding like a goody-goody, I feel hopeful and energized in terms of what's ahead for us.

A CRASH COURSE IN MANAGING TRIGGERS

We all want to feel indispensable, especially in tough and unpredictable times. It gives us the sense that we have some control over our future. *Fortune* magazine recently reported that white collar employees are working longer hours than usual, winding up over-committed and overscheduled. Because of the times, it said, "people are troweling on extra effort," hoping it will help them keep their jobs. The rationale is, "If I've got this many projects under way, they can't fire me, right?"

If effort, commitment and loyalty meant that we could stop disruptive change within a company, we'd all be employed. Instead, the smartest use of energy is to...

> ➤ observe your surroundings.
> ➤ stay informed about your industry.
> ➤ manage your emotions.
> ➤ plan your strategy for survival—either you stay where you are or move to another.
> ➤ heed the triggers.

Take a closer look:

> ➤ **What are the facts?** Compare the trends and events in your industry with the subtle and dramatic changes that have begun to occur in your immediate work environment. Can you predict a trigger across the board? Have a few gone off in your company that have not affected you—yet? Start putting two and two together.
>
> ➤ **Prepare for the shock of the news.** Be aware. If triggers have gone off, give yourself, at the most, two or three days to grieve, feel panic or betrayal, then make your plans. If you're going to be lifetime employable, you must think of yourself as proactive, not reactive. To live in total denial puts you at risk.

Change may be unwelcome as the earthquake unsettling the west coast, but it has come. Wishing it were yesterday, unfissured earth and houses standing, won't make it so. A trigger may be painful and disruptive, but it's easier to deal with it, survive and prosper when you face it as soon as possible.

Then again, is the news all bad? Look for the positive side.

What's your investment in this job? If rumors, facts and attitude add up to imminent change, clarify what you want from your job and what it means to you. This can be the most sensitive issue to handle. If a trigger is about to go off, ask yourself a few tough questions.

The practical side: What direction are you taking your career? Are you loyal to the company or a person or group of people—boss, mentor, your "team"? What does this company have that you can find someplace else—can you go out and win at "company musical chairs." If a disruptive trigger goes off and it means a layoff, are you ready for it?

The emotional side: Are you "looking for love in all the wrong places?" Are you overly emotionally invested in your job, transferring your needs from the traditional family structure to a company? Large companies tend to paternalistic style and the child in us responds to that. Is the company where a lot of your needs are met: acceptance, acknowledgment, influence, power, affection, continuity, a stabilizing force, where you turn to for definition and security?

The company you're with even at its worst provides a semblance of continuity and human contact. One result is that we may refuse to believe the worst—"expulsion" from the family, or job loss. But most people resist change over which they have little control and fight for what they have, often by denial.

Life is a series of events, some of which you can influence while others just sweep over you. Sometimes change comes at you like a broadside accident. Things will end one way or another, even a job. But take action!

FINALLY

While it's true that the better performers with keener skills (including interpersonal ones) tend to survive over all over, even they cannot fully control their destiny in these times. But they have a definite edge. How do they handle triggers? What strategies do they use to stay in? Who remains and why? How do some make themselves more "indispensable" than others? It starts with who you want to work with, how they support you and how you work with others. Your own good attitude and its management is a major advantage in career longevity.

Here's how.

WRAP-UP

➤ There are still companies today who are ignoring the triggers or signals of change. Many companies are not adapting fast enough or cling to the past—until outside events force change on them.

➤ The smart survivor needs to keep his or her antenna up for inevitable change in company life—and understand and overcome any resistance to it.

➤ Triggers tell you change is on its way—and it will come as a trend or an event.

➤ A trigger, when it's a trend, starts as a temporary measure, like temporary cutbacks or shifts in consumer tastes and demands. Trends allow you to be agile and mobile.

➤ A trigger, when it's an event, is sudden and irreversible and toss you into another realm, such as a takeover, a stock crash or a merger.

➤ Triggers differ but have three intrinsic qualities in common: the buzzing, or the rumor that change may occur, you then need to weigh the rumor against the facts, and the shock of awareness—the truth is out in the open.

4

ATTITUDE:
How Enlightened
Self-Management Keeps the Job

S *unday Morning*, on CBS, recently did a profile of the astonishing Selma Burke, a 94-year-old African-American sculptor whose award-winning portrait of Franklin Delano Roosevelt would eventually be memorialized on the U.S. dime.

Imagine the racial, sexual and cultural barriers a woman of color—who is also an artist—had to triumph over. As old as the century, Mrs. Burke is still carving stone and wood in her Philadelphia studio. The interviewer asked her a question posed to every maverick: "Didn't people warn you against being an artist? Didn't they tell you, 'You can never make a living from art!'"

"I never asked people!" she said, in a dazzlingly cheerful and confident tone. "I was born to be a sculptor and that's all there is to know."

Such self-knowledge and commitment eventually earned her a Ph.D. and the chance to study art in Europe with Henri Matisse and Aristide Maillol—a pretty good cast of "mentors" for any woman in any decade.

Selma Burke has one sort of talent, but let me assure you of this: talent in any field—whether it's organizing an office, selling shoes, creating a popular fast-food franchise, designing rocket systems or discovering a wonder drug—and getting the most career satisfaction out of it depends, first of all, on attitude.

Not luck.

Not connections.

Not being at the top of your class and being recruited into a top job at a Fortune 500 company.

It is attitude and fortitude that will get you through the changes and shifts in constant motion every day in the business world—motions over which you have no control. Remember, no company in the world can guarantee you continuous or lifetime employment. No matter how stable the company you work for seems right now, it will continue to restructure, outsource, merge and even let go of their best employees. The team, the boss, the management or the company you work for could change simply with a signature on a contract.

What can you do about it?

Simple: none of these facts of business life are personal, no matter how it may temporarily disrupt your career and your life. Worldwide shifts in how companies are run are facts of life. Unless you own the company or are buying one out, you cannot control organizational events.

What you can control, however, is how you feel, how you think about what transpires, and how you act. Your survival depends not so much on what happens to you, as on how you handle what happens.

If you're reading this book, you've probably experienced these changes. How can you manage them and win?

Attitude.

Smart self-management begins here.

KEEP A POSITIVE ATTITUDE

One psychological cost of a company shake-up may be a momentary drop in your self-affirmation—that sense of worth faltering in the face of potential financial and professional loss. Hit a crossroad, and your motivation to keep going can flag. Since you can't change events, you can change how you look at them.

Martin P. Seligman, Ph.D., a psychologist who wrote the interesting *What You Can Change and What You Can't,* commented that people are astonishingly attracted to the catastrophic interpretation of things. By "people" he meant not just neurotics, depressives, phobics or explosive personalities, but "most of us, most of the time."

Seligman stressed that the moods (or depressions) which can wreak havoc with our health can be cured by "straightforward changes in conscious thinking or helped by medication, but it cannot be cured by insight into childhood." What interests me is his focus on conscious thinking—the language we use to talk to ourselves about who we are and what's happened to us. Or, how we control thinking.

Optimism—or positive or proactive thinking—is simply a learned skill. Once you learn how to be optimistic, Seligman said, it "increases achievement at work and improves physical health."

It all makes sense!

Proactive attitudes like these let you focus on ends rather than means, clarify your judgment so you know which road to take, help you keep your energy up, reduce panic—and sustain your lifetime employability. A proactive attitude starts with knowing that you don't have to be perfect, you just have to play up your strengths, take a hard look at shortcomings and learn to put them aside.

"A positive attitude may not solve all your problems but it will annoy enough people to make it worthwhile," a friend sent me a greeting card with this message in it, and at first I thought, "Pretty corny!" The concept of positive thinking and a confident attitude may sound corny, but how much power does it really have?

A positive, productive attitude not only bestows on you real power, but it will:

➤ help you reinforce a sense of personal control and reverse emotional downswings—depression, anger, malingering, fatalism or the urge to drop out.

➤ help you expect change and be flexible in dealing with it.

➤ help you listen for and look for opportunities and not get swept away in panic by the company's new direction.

➤ help you be more tolerant of management mistakes! You may not know all the reasons for change and what they're planning to do about it.

➤ help you be enthusiastic or openly willing to familiarize yourself or adapt to a change before taking it personally.

➤ help you control the psychological aspects of change in your

work place without your frustrations affecting productivity.
Streamlining companies will seek out people who can
negotiate, run meetings and function under stress. They're
less likely to keep on or promote complainers.

➤ help you be sensitive to people around you. The work place
is a round robin. The person who's your boss today may
be asking you for a job next week! You can't afford not to
be considerate. The old way of working is obsolete.

To clarify how you feel about change and how you fit in
your work place, ask yourself:

➤ Do you think working in a large company is more likely to
guarantee employment than a small one?

➤ Has your productivity gone down sharply because you are
worried, depressed, insecure or caught in a new power
game because of changes?

➤ Has your productivity gone up because changes have
improved your position and how the company is
structured?

➤ Who do you report to and what is your relationship with
that person? Have you felt any shifts in attitude lately from
that person?

WHEN YOU'RE SUDDENLY IN
THE GAME OF MUSICAL CHAIRS

The one-job-in-a-lifetime formula no longer suits the economic, social,
attitudinal and realistic career patterns of the 1990s. Statistics remind
us that the average person—a perfectly respectable, responsible, skilled
person like you—will probably have 10.5, not 1.5, jobs in a lifetime.
"Musical chairs," another way of describing job change, sometimes
doesn't feel like a jolly walk from one seat to the next. But understand
what you're going through, adopt a proactive attitude, and job change
will mean change for the better.

Let's start when, metaphorically, the music's started. You learn your company is cutting back, merging, relocating, downsizing, or setting a change in motion that points to a reorganization that may or may not include you. In the first shock waves of change:

➤ uncertainty and ambiguity strike.

➤ you start searching for information on what will happen next.

➤ you get vague responses from higher-ups on who, what, where and how.

➤ then you know: you're in or you're out!

The first time you're let go or the company falls to pieces so everyone goes, it's a gut-wrenching experience. "Beyond what you can bear," Sarah West*, a children's wear designer said emphatically, when the garment company she worked for moved to the Philippines:

> The job and the company was just a good fit for me. Ten years with almost the same people. It wasn't just the end of a great job, it was also the breakup of a family. Where would I ever find another shop with that kind of magic?

Creative, organizational or technological though your specialty may be, people like Sarah who are used to a well-defined job with clear policies and procedures are often the most shook up with the news of a job termination. When structure is pulled out from under you, you reel. Hopefully, not for long. What you do immediately following the news of a job loss depends on temperament—you either act or react:

Maybe you think bravado is the answer in a last-ditch battle to win a power game, or at least get your licks in. Perhaps the quick getaway that shortens the pain cycle is your answer: you pack up your desk, but not before you openly voice hurt feelings.

Maybe in a sober but emotion-filled flurry of activity you, like Sarah West, line up as many job interviews as possible and get a first-hand overview of the market and the competition. And another job with more of a future. Or as with A.J. (Tony) Yadonga, you go through a wide range of feelings starting with panic and become preoccupied with survival.

Tony, who is now a director of human resources of Zenith Laboratories in New Jersey, talked to me about the first time the company he worked for closed around him. He felt a foreboding uncertainty for the future where all he could think about was his obligations, his dental plan, taking care of his children, the grief of losing his job. Then came the anger. Tony heard himself bad-mouthing the now-defunct company and his boss, telling his tale of woe. Then he found the right job and life was good again.

Years later, that company folded. Though Tony's first reaction was to think, "I can't believe this is happening to me again," his sense of proportion was modified. The steps he took to get work were more sure-footed, less fueled by panic and more strategic. He worked on building a network for himself of contacts so he wasn't so much at bay. He began slowly, knowing other people were in the same position as he was; at least, he said, he could "call someone and see what was out there." He told me:

> I hadn't really focused on maintaining contacts because I'd landed in this second company, and it seemed unnecessary. So much for foresight.
>
> Losing my job the second time drove home a big truth: if you forget that "musical chairs" are going to happen, you get lulled into a sense of false security. You'll probably change chairs again and again, so this is just the way it is.
>
> We're part of this high state of flux. You don't own the desk, you rent it and you pay your rent by performance and behavior.

What Tony learned the second time out was how to uncover the possibilities by being part of a network, and by accepting the fact that job change thrust upon you may well be inevitable—and work well in your favor! By the time of his third job change, Tony's network counted about 500 people. Many of them came to him through the church group he joined, using his skills in human resources to advise and help others. His commitment to helping others not only gained him a vast network, but he's learned to be respectful toward people and they toward him.

Know that if you're suddenly a player in musical chairs, you can best approach change this way:

➤ control your emotions
➤ ask yourself the right questions:

➤ Who are your contacts and your allies and how can you make others?

➤ Have you postponed action or is motivation blocked by procrastination or self-pity?

➤ Are you open to feedback?

➤ Are you making use of the new rules of the '90s, that is for one, no longer think like an employee but an entrepreneur.

➤ shape circumstance or be its victim, and,

➤ know that wait-and-see attitudes put you at a disadvantage

➤ be proactive, not reactive. Keep moving and get that seat!

How do you respond to small changes on the job? Are you:

➤ analytical at first, then easily adaptable?

➤ jittery?

➤ quietly off balance but with a quick recovery?

➤ so interested, you even see how to improve the changes?

➤ hyper-alert to your work environment and prefer the status quo?

➤ spending more time with colleagues discussing rumors and changes than getting down to business?

➤ making no decision until you've searched out the facts of the change and all ambiguities are cleared up?

LISTEN TO CRITICISM

Except, of course, for the shock of being fired, almost nothing in the work place I can think of is more likely to shatter the status quo, egos, (or even careers), than criticism. It's unsettling to be on the receiving end of criticism from co-workers or employers who suggest you're not fulfilling your duties or their idea of what's expected of you.

Criticism comes in as many styles as there are personalities delivering it, such as:

➤ "Your numbers are really off this month, Jeff. Let's meet later today—we can talk and look things over."

➤ "You always set yourself up as the perfect person and talk to us like we're dummies! Guess what, Joanne—you're a bully, and a joke of a manager at that!"

➤ "I can always count on you for a really so-so job, Fred."

No matter how fair the approach, few of us want to know our "numbers are off" in any interpretation of the meaning relating to work. And even if the critic has the "right" to criticize us or believes the criticism is kindly gesture for our own good, the experience is unpleasant.

Take my three examples.

Only one approach is reasonable and makes you willing to re-evaluate your work and make changes: the first case. Here, the speaker is direct, lets Jeff know the point of the criticism is based on recent results; the speaker is willing to hear what may be affecting Jeff's performance.

In the second case, the speaker is angry at Joanne now and from a backlog of prior frustrating interactions with her; the attack stance is bound to further the antagonism and keep the department pivoting around the relationship between rival personalities, rather than upon meeting goals.

In the third case, the speaker is hostile and sarcastic, demeaning Fred by implying he's always inadequate; the speaker doesn't offer a chance to discuss improvement, but sets up a situation where Fred would probably use whatever time he can take with the speaker to defend himself. For all we know, Fred is always topnotch, but the speaker begrudges him his abilities.

In example one, the approach makes ideas and opinions accessible to the other. The second and third example are counter-productive and pain-inflicting. If fate should deliver you to the receiving end of such words, change the nature of the criticism.

Coolly face your critic, then ask for the specifics of why you're not hitting the mark and what is required of you and how. Do not ever let anyone comment adversely on your work in a general way, only to shut off further communication. Play to your advantage, do not give in to a disadvantage set up by others. Once you get the information from your critic, think it over. Is there any truth in the evaluation? If so, offer to correct the situation or change your behavior.

Another point to consider about criticism: when are you getting it? Is it business as usual or is it dealt out during a corporate changeover—a cutback, downsizing, a new manager, a new location, and so on.

People at every level feel pressured during changeovers; they worry and become confused about how they'll be evaluated, and by whom. Are they good, good enough, not good? Maybe more confusing and anxiety-making, they suddenly don't know whose scale to use in evaluating themselves in terms of performance and potential. The situation itself makes people poke at each other.

Tirer le maximum, so the French saying goes, which wisely advises, make the most of what you have. Apply this basic principle to any area relating to your work, including criticism: rather than brood over what you aren't or what other people may or may not think of you, pull yourself together, strategize and maximize what you are.

"Don't get mad, get ahead," said psychologist, Adele Scheele, author and former columnist for *Working Woman* magazine—equally good advice.

ADMIT YOUR MISTAKES AND MOVE ON

What if you're your own worst critic!

If so, you get bogged down in worrying what others think of you. Since you want to be perfect, to make a mistake is tantamount to a professional Hiroshima. You tend to create a worst-case scenario and turn it into a self-fulfilling prophesy—you fall from "friendly fire," dropping your own bombs on your own territory. Or, if you are obsessive about being perfect, you may recite a litany of "if onlys" until you're rendered ineffectual.

Everyone makes mistakes. Everyone. But too often, people go to creative lengths to try and hide errors or make someone else responsible for them. A mistake—by omission or commission, or not knowing the answer and improvising one—brings with it a fear of embarrassment once the mistake or (misinformation) is discovered.

The smartest professional move is to admit to it. Give a reason or explanation for the mistake, but not an excuse; then tell how you plan to fix it. The quicker you amend a problem, the more respect you gain from colleagues and superiors.

"I got into the habit of not signing off on certain memos requesting certain meetings or briefs, especially if I knew I wasn't prepared to sit down at the table," Carl, a corporation lawyer once told me. "That way, if someone above me came down on me for something I didn't do, I'd say I never got the memo. They'd check and see I was telling the truth...no signature."

Carl's game served him well for about a year, until the vice president he reported to got wise and made him own up. "I was testing to see how far I could go. Suddenly, my job was on the line."

Or, let's say you accidentally shipped an extra five cases of grommets to Smyth's, Inc. instead of Smythe's and Company, both important accounts.

Although your instinct may be to protect yourself and deny any knowledge of the error, adjust your thinking. Stay calm and take responsibility for your problem shipment. Panic is no excuse for blaming others ("If Penny kept the computer files in better shape, I wouldn't have hit the wrong key for Smythe!") or using the "victim defense" ("No one ever tells me anything around this office. Besides, you know I can't spell.").

Employers aren't interested in self-serving excuses—it costs them money, long-term clients and reputations. Professionals own up to errors and use the time and energy to rectify mistakes, rather than whine. ("I spoke to the guys at Smythe and Company about the one-day delay, and overnighted their full order. Also, I checked the wrong Smythe's accounts for the last three years and see that they order six cases from us every fall. I'll call and explain the error and see if they can store the extra five cases that went out. If not, I'll arrange for a pick up...")

Whether it's a mistake in judgment or a mistake in work performance, see yourself as your client, your superior or your critic sees you. What really did you do? Can it be corrected without losing time or money, so your company or the client feels they aren't overpaying for the same service?

Who would you prefer to work with? The person who whines or the person who makes things happen?

Take a closer look at your confidence level on the job to see if you are opening yourself up to change. Are you:

➤ willing to take risks?

➤ discrete about what you say and to whom you say it?

➤ double- and triple-checking on underlings work?

➤ protecting your territory but not limiting your upward mobility?

➤ finally dropping a conservative or isolationist stance and becoming more team-oriented and less disoriented.

➤ distancing yourself from co-workers who spend an inordinate amount of time interpreting superior's actions?

➤ extending yourself beyond the 9-5 mentality and willing to go the extra mile?

SYNTHESIZE SPECIFIC SKILLS

If you were at a cocktail party in another city, how would you introduce yourself to the person standing next to you? Are you likely to extend a hand and say, "I'm the senior manager of the loan division of the Triple Y Bank in Convex, Massachusetts. Oh! Hi! I'm Arlene Smith." Or do you say, "G. G. Jones...Hope and Jones Insurance. Chickpea, Texas." Or simply, "Winnie Smith. Glad to meet you!"

Sometimes, I'm surprised at how intensely our identities are tied up in the work we do. "He's a doctor," means status in every sense of the word to the person who admires the profession or covets its general social and economic rewards. "Doctor" can mean charlatan to another person who believes totally in alternate healing practices. And what about the doctor: what does he think of himself? Does he have any interests other than his practice and can he talk about them?

What about you? How do you think about yourself? Are you the job you have at the moment and does it totally define you, or do you look at the totality that is your whole life? You have personality. Character. Humor. Hobbies. Life experiences. Everything you've learned and done makes up what you are. Don't leave this self-knowledge at the reception desk when you walk down the corridor to your desk.

Past experience is not simply memories: It could influence your future on the job.

I know a crackerjack administrative assistant, who in her other life was a chef, who studied cooking and restaurant management in Europe. Carrie* took a job—she thought temporarily—with a huge advertising firm when she didn't get the position she wanted at the restaurant she preferred. She heard her boss on the phone trying to line up a new caterer for a Christmas party, and an idea struck her.

When she got home, Carrie set up a menu and budget for the party. The next day, she asked for a minute of her boss's time and, after telling him about her cooking experience in Europe, she made an offer: She would like to handle all their receptions and business parties for a set fee. They agreed, assured that she'd deliver. Carrie, who knew she would satisfy her "client's" needs, was immediately transformed into an "intrapreneur"—someone who runs a department that functions as an individual profit center within a larger company structure.

Planning a party may not be within the job description of "administrative assistant," but having the courage to exploit a skill beyond the limit of a job is smart self-management. Carrie's interests, abilities and knowledge paid off well.

A proactive attitude is never more visible than when you apply it directly to exercising and improving skills. Carrie knew an opportunity when she heard one and jumped. Like her, use a general knowledge of the business you're in to concentrate on what you do best beyond your job description—and let others know what that is. Highlight and enhance the skills that are most applicable to your company's future business.

Do you have a talent for organization, trouble-shooting, scheduling, time management? Use it all! Ask yourself how your company would most benefit if...production were streamlined by eliminating two workers at step C who'd be better used at step D, where production slows up, and so on?

Now is the time to get those credentials—certificates, degrees or licenses that you take with you. It's very possible that your company will offer to help pay for schooling or training. Amazingly, only a tiny fraction of employees take advantage of programs offered. They say they're too busy or too stressed or too tired after work to extend the day and sit in a classroom.

If your company is happy to help improve their employee's skills and pay for it, sign up! This is your chance. Invest in yourself by giving time and interest—you can sleep or take those extra hours after work for leisure after you get the credentials you need.

Synthesize life skills!

GIVE YOURSELF A PLACE TO BLOW OFF STEAM OUTSIDE OF YOUR WORK PLACE

"Twenty or thirty years ago, the executive tantrum had a lot of power," a women's magazine editor told me. She even read advice in another magazine about how once a month you should explode with just enough force to let people know you took your job seriously and didn't take guff!

An advertising account executive said something similar:

> Sometimes anger is about literally nothing but pushing someone else around. I used to work at an agency where the president of the company got a kick out of threatening art directors. The man would throw their work against the walls and tell them they were no-talent idiots!
>
> We all thought of it as a Hitler complex—you know, the failed artist becoming a monster tyrant and attacking people who could do what he couldn't.

Francine Greeley*, an administrator in a New York sporting goods company, told me:

> My boss is very smart and she knows the business, but she's got two real flaws that make me want to quit this job. Whatever anyone else does, she undoes. Whatever you suggest that may be important and operative, she vetoes in a condescending manner. Then lo and behold, you hear your suggestions coming out of her mouth at a staff meeting, while she takes credit for your work! She's a vampire! She drains the life out of us. It makes me so mad just to come to work now.

How should either of these women respond? Ignore a boss's tactics and look for another position in the company, or another job elsewhere? Should she retaliate in kind—that is, fight it out?

Anger, histrionics and games of vengeance have no real long-term benefit in the work place. Suffering a calculating boss is a job in itself, but you can do something about it.

First up is to analyze the corporate culture. Do such "vampiric" strategies exist easily within the company? Is the culture compatible with your style and values? Next, meet with your boss and lay your concerns on the table—and do so with tact. If you get more condescension or anger in response, then you can make your decision to stay or go.

Francine dislikes the culture and her boss, but she realizes that the company provides something she needs in her career: they offer an invaluable opportunity for her to take on a wide range of responsibilities beyond her job description. She knows she's got to put in a few years there before she goes elsewhere at a much higher level. Meanwhile, she learned to face the demons.

There's the entrepreneurial side to conflict of personalities, too: being in business for yourself also means controlling your temper with valued clients who may also be difficult. You want to keep your customers, but how do you control yourself when your inclination is to explode?

I learned a technique from Dr. Yvette Obadia, a New York psychoanalyst who suggests "the three-minute whine"—a period to let off steam within a timed limit. You set an egg timer or alarm clock for three minutes, go into a room alone, focus on the subject of your anger and moan, groan, blame, yowl, throw papers or burst into tears...until the bell goes off.

Once the time is up, stop, put aside any residue of anger and resume business as usual—cleansed.

I first used it a few years ago, when I was obsessing over a client who was demanding of my time. He called three or four times a day to chew over the same issues, complaining at every step, making outrageous demands for changes in reports. Working with him was a chore.

I turned to the timer a few times a day after those phone calls with him, and I thought, what can I do? I valued him as a client and didn't want to lose his business, but he was pushing me to the edge. It soon occurred to me that most of his complaints had little to do with my work or the reality of the project.

Rather, unable to vent anger at his own company, he used me and our relationship to let off steam. He knew I wouldn't yell back at him or jeopardize our agreement, but he didn't know what I had to do to maintain my cool: the timer.

A second option is to have a support team to whom you can moan and groan. I have three friends with a strong sense of self, a sober perspective on life and business sense who are willing to listen to my complaints, ease me out of anger and make me laugh. While they don't make the difficulties go away, they can put me in a better frame of mind to improve my attitude.

CREDENTIALS AND THE "A" STUDENT COMPLEX

I was talking to a high-energy 34-year-old merchandising executive who had just been let go after a huge wave of cutbacks at a department store. Jack* had been out of work just three days and preoccupied with one thought: who would hire him and should he lie about his academic credentials. He said:

> I had a job interview yesterday, and the guy asked me what I thought was my strong point and my weak spot. I can really think on my feet—my strong point—and give you solutions to problems, one after the other.
>
> My weak spot is I never finished college and I know it's a factor in how high I can go. What bothers me is I know I'm street smart, and can make it pay off, but I don't kid myself. I have rough edges. Am I going to be the guy they hire and promote? Am I going to be the guy they head-hunt for the title?

One of the youngest billionaires in America attended college for one year, but quit to start a business with a friend. The company eventually changed America's relationship to computers. The man is Bill Gates and his company, Microsoft. Gates is unique and other talented and lucky entrepreneurs may know an equally graced fate. But my first order of advice would be to not quit school after a year.

So, what Jack has in common with Gates, other than one year of college, is drive and originality. Jack, though, puts too much store in the power of a certificate, and undersells himself and his experience in business.

Finishing college has its merits, but, its paradoxical opposite—playing the "A student" as your professional style—may hold you back from career advancement as surely as can self-devaluation from a lack of credentials. Stan Herlinger*, is an example of what I mean.

Stan graduated from college with honors and got his M.B.A. from an ivy league school. Stan was a champ at memorizing and regurgitating facts. Recruited on campus by a large not-for-profit organization, which needed a smart, numbers person in their accounting office, Stan turned out to be a good assistant who followed orders—he did his job and got steady raises for four years. When his superior left, Stan was promoted to the man's job. He told me what happened next:

> I did everything right to get that promotion. I knew I could take over and run the department by the book like I thought they wanted. I never overstepped the line.
>
> A year later, they called me in to tell me they'd hired an outside guy over me! Someone they thought could bring in more business. Not that they were completely unhappy with me. They said I could stay at a different level but I felt like a jerk.
>
> I don't get it! How can you do everything right and still get bad marks?

Stan was smart, competent; he knew the rules, followed orders and was a company man. To put it in language Stan understands, he couldn't figure out why he "wasn't getting an 'A' from them." He was doing what had to be done. Unfortunately, Stan's frame of reference wasn't the nature of business, but the procedures that make good students.

One of the problems of those who are very good in school, is that they become passive.

The behavioral qualities that make up the "A" student are passivity, memory of facts and theories, mannerly interrogation, doing what your teacher tells you to. After a cool and confident manner in the face of test taking, you go home and wait for your grade. If you did everything right, you get your "A."

This was Stan at school and on the job. Like the good student, he learned what he needed to get the job done (or his version of "reading the book for the course"), made no waves by being innovative or asking provocative questions (or his version of being an attentive student who doesn't challenge authority). He said:

> I saw my friends scrambling from place to place and job to job. I was sure it wasn't just industries in trouble, but people who didn't know how to fit in. I was sure that if I followed the rules, I'd be rewarded with no need to do much else.

So let's look at Jack, with one year of college and a better intuitive sense of business. Jack didn't get his jollies from high grades in school as Stan did. Along the way, Jack had to be more enterprising—even in school, where he was more the B and C student. He had to apply other interpersonal skills to get by—such as chatting up the teacher. "C-students," a corporate head hunter told me, "are often more entrepreneurial because they've always had to learn other ways around."

Once, C-students were not recruited out of school by the big corporations; they were considered people who literally did not make the grade. They didn't fit into a bureaucracy because they were considered the hustlers, the mavericks or the outsiders, not the stars. In an interesting turn of events, corporations began to seek in new recruits the very qualities that were considered out of favor, out of the mainstream and a bit suspect 10 years ago.

The desirable traits companies look for now are the ability to move, change, and think entrepreneurially. What was once considered "flighty" is now admired as "flexible."

I'm not suggesting that any student slack off or not achieve academically while in school. My advice is far more practical: Take the best of the A-student attitude to work with you—being a quick study at knowing your job or where to get important information—and leave the drawbacks of the good student behind, especially passivity.

"There is very little difference in people. But that little difference makes a big difference. The little difference is attitude, the big difference is whether it is positive or negative."

W. CLEMENT STONE,
motivational author and entrepreneur

ENTITLEMENT ENDS HERE!

"I've been here since day one. How can they fire me?"

"I've got an M.B.A. and connections. I should be promoted before anyone. I'm not giving three years to this company unless I get a title first!"

"My department couldn't function without me."

Sound familiar?

These are three variations on a theme that doesn't fly in the work place any longer—entitlement. What does that mean exactly?

It may be that: You put in your time and for that you expect to be paid, to enjoy the perks (health insurance, bonuses, retirement package, certain expenses, and more), praised when you do well—and a yearly raise that means something.

It may be that: You believe that because you earned credentials, are a woman or a minority, have social connections or work for a large, fairly stable corporation or in a civil service job that you should be singled out for special treatment or exist in your career, at your desk until retirement, immune from the shocks of business world changes.

The concept of the permanent or entitled employee has gone the way of the quill pen: it's more a quaint artifact than a working instrument in today's market. The structure of business has changed too much to feel complacent, limited within the job description or entitled to lifetime care by the company.

Cliff Hakim, in his book *We're All Self-Employed,* acknowledges one dilemma workers have always faced: the issue of strongly identifying with one's job, so it's a major part of themselves. However, as organizations are reshaped, workers must be reshaped too and identities altered. The employer-employee contract, once taken for granted, is simply undermined.

He said:

> Dependence is the key feature of this agreement and created entitlement.... Today our world is summoning us toward independence and interdependence—core elements of a new social contract.
>
> Collaboration is a primary characteristic of interdepen-

dence, the ability to share what you know and to integrate information from others—teamwork.

The employer/employee entitlement relationship puts all the responsibility on the employer to provide for the employee. It set up a situation where the employee thinks, "I'm appropriately performing my daily tasks, so the company appropriately owes me."

And its affect on you? How do you do the most for yourself? Hakim goes on to say:

> ...If from this very moment you begin to develop a self-employed attitude by attending to your own personal and professional development and by thinking how your skills, values and interests could be relevant to customer...
>
> We are all workers no matter what we do. Our focus needs to be on initiation and contribution, not on subservience— the suppression of self and ideas.

Or, taking on an autonomous mind set. You may work in a company, but now you must think in terms of how your department can function as a unit, centered on giving service and being a profit center. You're part of a team, but you still have to be out for yourself.

You now need to recommit yourself to your job every chance you get. If your job description changes, don't waste time bemoaning the changes, but see the change as an opportunity to learn more. Prepare for change and a change in your attitude.

An attitude of entitlement lessens emotional and professional rewards and limits the number of opportunities and how you will achieve. Entitlement's got within it a bit of "A student" mentality—that "I'm being good!" pleaser's motivation. Instead, your best chances for getting the most from your career is to adopt a proactive attitude, and that is the new reality:

Client-centered thinking.

In a nutshell, client centering means that as an employee you treat your company not like a boss, but like a client. Where's the benefit in that? You're more on your toes, thinking like your competitors or outside consultants and bringing more to the company. I'll talk about how this process works and what it can do for your career, next, in Chapter Five.

Meanwhile, let's look at a truth about the employment picture and how a proactive attitude will help you move on, coming up next.

WRAP-UP

➤ A committed attitude and fortitude will get you through changes and shifts at work where before you felt you had no control.

➤ Your survival depends not so much on what happens to you as how you handle what happens.

➤ Smart self-management has the following elements: a positive attitude where you can change your interpretation by consciously thinking optimistically.

➤ Proactive thinking—where you surmount blows, strategize, and act on your plans—increases productivity, achievement and enthusiasm for work. Reactive thinking—where you did not get what you wanted and feel either entitled or victimized—insures that you will remain in employment limbo, going nowhere.

➤ A positive attitude gives you real power by helping you reinforce personal control, anticipate change, and be more flexible.

➤ You enhance your chances at work when you look and listen for opportunities, are more tolerant of management mistakes, deal with psychological change in your work place and listen to criticism coolly.

➤ You are more than your job title: You are the sum total of your experiences, personality and aspirations.

5

WHAT YOU NEED TO KNOW TO STAY SMART, STAY IN AND GET AHEAD

J im Booth*, a tall, 28-year-old Minnesota man whose career has been devoted to working with people who have a difficult time getting employed, such as displaced homemakers, school drop-outs and ex-convicts, recently had an epiphany. The agency he works for suffered when funding was cut two years ago, and he feared for his job security. But two years later he was at his desk, and with a promotion.

"Damn, I'm still here," he said to himself when a second wave of cuts trimmed the agency again, but didn't threaten his position. For a moment, he felt awe at being spared, even grateful. Then in a flash, he woke up. A thought occurred to him: "If I leave, it would be a tremendous loss for the agency because I'm so valuable! I'm the guy who knows how to sell our clients! I'm the guy who trains everyone who's hired!"

At that moment, Jim shifted the connection to security from "the company" to himself.

Other issues swayed Bonnie Maitlen, now a senior vice president of Professional Development at an international career management agency. A dynamic brunette in her 30s from the heartland of Indiana, Bonnie made her decision to leave her job and become an entrepreneur.

Let down from hitting a plateau and not doing more satisfying work, her 60-hour week, especially with having to care for a new baby, was grueling. Her own business seemed to be the solution, but Bonnie wasn't a one-man band. She talked her boss into quitting his job, she quit hers, and with a third partner, they started a research and training firm with an investment of $1,000 each.

Jim and Bonnie opted for different career paths, but both of them determined their value at "the company"—with Jim, not only was he a capable leader, so was he a coach, a client-centered thinker and a proactive manager. He decided to stay on with his agency. Bonnie, also a proactive thinker and client-centered manager, thought she could best use her skills jumping off the plateau and into her own business— taking co-workers with her on the venture.

Jim and Bonnie have many qualities in common: foremost is that they possess a high proactive standard that will always give them an edge in the 1990s changing company. More important, neither one thinks like a middle manager, but like a senior person, and acts on those ideals.

Jim told me:

> People tend to turn their power over to a situation at work and then feel they have no control. They think, "I can't do anything about things here, I don't know where this organization is going and then undervalue themselves." I did it myself.
>
> I know what I can do, I know how to ask the right questions and who I have to ask. And if my job ends tomorrow, I'm confident I have the skill set, the flexibility and the drive to find something else.

And Bonnie: After writing proposals to the organizations they'd worked with at their previous jobs, Bonnie and her partners came up with a grant that provided the minimal amount of cash they needed to swing the company. Bonnie explained:

> I was never a risk taker, but this move taught me that I could take a risk. I was always looking for security, but when we got that first grant, I became more confident. Tenacious. I wanted to balance my work priorities with my personal life. That inner drive to make it work, just worked.

> I think the biggest gift we could give to people is to help
> them shift job security from a company to themselves and
> not be the victim of circumstance.

In her own company for a few years, she's grown enormously, creating more options for herself on a managerial level. She's invested a lot of herself in reading about trends in her field of organizational development, improving her skills and assimilating what she's learned and using it in discussion pieces to pitch clients. She also collects books and attends seminars on change and empowerment, as she says, so that she "understands them, even if I'm not training people on those topics. But change and empowerment are the topics affecting organizations I work with."

Jim and Bonnie are two examples of how achievement-oriented people are acknowledging specific changes and dealing with them now. These changes—which affect you, too—are:

> ➤ hitting a plateau.
> ➤ turning to client-centered thinking.
> ➤ thinking content instead of context.
> ➤ shifting from the idea of "the Lone Ranger" to team player.
> ➤ tuning into the importance of coaching (training or mentoring) others, or to be open to such learning.

Let's look closer at what you need to know about these issues to best serve your future:

#1: MAKING PEACE WITH THE PLATEAU

In a cartoon called, "The Glass Floor," *New Yorker* cartoonist Roz Chast captured an ironic moment in the life of one female executive pondering the fate of her job. Rather than worry about the limitations of the "glass ceiling"—looking up to the top positions with great aspirations— this woman is sitting behind a big desk with a slightly perilous-looking "glass floor" under her, thinking, "Maybe if I just sit very, very still, nothing will happen."

Chast probably meant this cartoon to describe a woman on the way out and in a fervent state of denial. However, the sketch reminded me of a far less terminal state of work and its attendant feelings: that hold-your-breath-and-it-will-all-go-away attitude that occurs when you hit a plateau on the job. And because you've plateaued, you worry, unbefittingly, that you will henceforth sit very still while nothing happens!

Plateaus need not signal stasis, but progress! Flat though they may be, plateaus have possibilities, interest and, by changing your outlook, a new vista. A jump off a plateau to your own venture, as with Bonnie Maitlen, is not the only solution for change.

Of the many concerns I've heard from people about promotions, success or job satisfaction, one of the most worrisome is knowing the position/title you hold may never change appreciably. A twelfth vice president of international loans at one bank may switch jobs to eighth vice president at another—and never make it to president, CFO or CEO.

And curse the plateau.

So, what, really, is the plateau all about?

There are a few definitions: "People who plateau reach a stage in their lives or careers and can't see any way to reach the next step. Plateaus equals stoppage," a 34-year-old architectural draftsman from Boston told me.

Then there's a second demarcation where plateauing is more than a defeatist attitude that you can't go any further, it is fact. "I'm at a company where more and more people plateau because there's no place, or fewer places, for us to rise to. People at the top have plateaued, too. The climb is over!" an advertising account executive at a New York agency said.

In some cases, as with this advertising agency, the organization isn't honest with its employees about the long-term possibilities. That's another fact. Why deceive you? If you're good, they want to hire you—and incentives, like promotion, are alluring.

The urge to upward mobility is very real, but with a plateau, very squelched. When our expectations demand ever-increasing success, we're disappointed as far fewer of us experience the joy of promotion. Instead, we feel "flattened" and part of the flattening process occurring in companies—yet most of us don't understand why we fail to reach higher levels.

Plateaus tend to remind people of a place to stop climbing and, therefore, they shrug off challenges. The truth is that most of us will plateau at some time in our lives or our work. So how are you going to make a life for yourself if you do not want to move laterally or leave?

The trick is to become proactive when you level off; seal up any cracks in a glass floor you may have manufactured for yourself—and turn the plateau into a free range of discovery!

Note Don Anderson's* case.

Don, a brawny 32-year-old middle manager in a textile manufacturing plant, has been with his company for 12 years. Don quit college in his junior year "to get a jump on his career" through practical experience, and eventually got his degree in night school. He thought of himself as a "company man in a company town," and his future, he thought, looked as rich as the tapestry fabrics that came off the looms. He told me:

> For a while I got promoted every couple of years, then it slowed down. Now it's six years since the last one. I guess I better face it—maybe there's one more promotion, maybe there's no more. Too bad things aren't like they were 20 years ago, when moving up seemed easier.
>
> I wonder if my perception of myself is the same as others. I think I have a lot more to offer.

Don was caught in what Judith Bardwick, Ph.D., author of *The Plateauing Trap*, a fascinating study of the phenomenon, calls the "structural plateau," which signals the temporary end of promotions. A stoppage like this is part of business history—it's always been true as long as there were employers and employees on salary. Now plateaus are blocking people earlier in their careers—and much sooner than what they're prepared for, striking at four or six years, instead of 20. Naturally, a few stars in the organization will keep going up and over walls, but most of us will have to endure structural plateau at one time in our careers.

One of the problems of the structural plateau is that, like Don Anderson, self-doubt gets a strong grip around the ego. Self-esteem is lost in proportion to the lack of satisfaction from a job.

What's the strategy to manage a structural plateau? At this point, you can decide if you want your life to have no momentum or if you want to create new opportunities and redefine your goals. Pete Riley*, a manager at a Birmingham manufacturing plant accounting firm, told me about how plateauing helped him redefine himself:

I don't mean I wouldn't like to become the general manager here—I would! I made peace with the fact that it isn't in the cards for me. I finally stopped chasing the job and started doing other things instead. Like improving myself.

The result is I do my work better than ever and I like it. I also took up tennis and play a few times a week. I've joined an investment club and generally have more time with friends and my wife. My life is good.

By accepting the structural plateau, and deciding to stay with this company rather than look elsewhere, Pete's found balance in his life, in and out of the office. He added:

I'm going to commit myself to my work and not anticipate moving. If it happens and I get the job, great. Now, I'm asking for other assignments, seeing what's in the company that I can learn. And that's okay.

I don't feel I'm giving up. Just being realistic.

Pete's attitude may yet get him the job he dreams of. He's still growing, demonstrating to his company that he's willing to take on other assignments, increasing his experience and skills. Pete would not fare as well within this company had he hit what Judith Bardwick, in her book, calls content plateauing, which very simply signals the end of the challenge. Or what you might also call, "burnout."

There are fewer reasons to despair of work than when the challenge is gone, and you continue, day after day, with work you've already mastered, never expanding on tasks or seeing new ways to invention or innovation. "I'll tell you what it's like," Stephanie Franks* said, referring to a job as a paralegal in a small law office where there had been no mobility for three years. "You get to feel like the classic underachiever. You get to wonder what happened to the fire in your belly!" She continued:

The cases change, but not the work or the people or the vibes in the places, which is tense and competitive.

A friend at the office I eat lunch with said to me the other day, "Face it, we're just slaves. I made peace with being a work slave. Just drop your work on me and I'll grind it out."

I thought, God protect me from that thinking. Laura's dependable and competent and she doesn't make any trouble—and she's easy to ignore.

Her remark struck a deep nerve. I know I have more to offer. I have ideas. I won't wind up like Laura, a workaholic who feels sorry for herself! I know it now.

You'll really get into trouble if, like Laura, resignation hardens into passivity and you don't have the imagination to bring any content to the party. Doing your job assiduously is commendable, but unless you search for the challenge and expand on the tasks you're given, you remain easy to ignore on your plateau—no matter how hard you work.

Stephanie brought up a point about her co-worker—workaholism. Of all types that you'd find at the office, workaholics are the most vulnerable. Their real passion and self-esteem is found in work, and work is only arena in which they can feel successful. Since one form of success is measured by promotion, the workaholic stranded on a plateau perceives the landing as an ending—and they panic. Where's their reason to live?

If you are a "one-legged" person on a plateau, understand that working longer and working harder doesn't mean you have a better life with more prestigious promotions. It doesn't mean you should resign, take any better sounding, high-paying job or drop out and move to Bali. Here's something to think about:

Only *1 percent* of people in the world are on the fast track and make incredible or newsworthy careers for themselves. For the rest of us, there is a reality in business—that is, fewer top slots exist than did 10 years ago. Since there are fewer top slots, more of us will hit a plateau. Where does that take us?

Motivate yourself.

While on a plateau, create and engage in constant change, even though it may not be weighed toward a promotion. Create new ambitions, discipline yourself, train yourself out of passivity, improve your self-esteem, be patient with yourself and know that you, like everyone else, is in the same place.

You don't have to feel bad about your career—take the time while on a plateau to reevaluate what work means to you and what work is not about.

Continue to learn new skills and change your commitment to work.

This is a key challenge since work is no longer about moving up. You're no longer on the proverbial ladder; expect a different type of climb, different momentum as you plateau, go back around, to the side, up, plateau...almost like being on a roller coaster.

#2: THINK CONTEXT INSTEAD OF CONTENT

You hit a problem at work that seems so overwhelming you think you can never solve it. A report, the financing, keeping up with memos, tiresome detail work cutting into your time, an impossible employee—you'd say you need hip boots to slog through all the issues affecting work.

There's a clear path through those heretofore insurmountable problems: instead of bemoaning the content of each issue—whether it's how to sort through the information, getting the money, and so forth—put the issue, the project, the problem or the strategy in another context.

This is what I mean. When you have a problem or need to solve an issue or discuss it, distance yourself from it by objectifying it. Emphasizing its subjectivity binds you to it emotionally.

For example, take the issue of an ongoing personality clash with someone you work with. Notice how heavy emotional investment in content (as in the first example below) gets fewer results than a reasonable and sober distancing through context (the second):

> **Subjective view:** "I have this problem with the assistant buyer. She's driving me crazy so I can't get my work done."
>
> **Objective view:** "The assistant buyer's style is to find a reason to argue about anything, make her presence known and interfere with others' productivity. The best response is no response."
>
> **Subjective view:** "This report doesn't tell the true story! The manager is biased, took my figures and came to a stupid marketing conclusion and shortchanged my contributions!"
>
> **Objective view:** "There are four key issues in this report I'd like to discuss. I've prepared some notes and pulled some figures that I think can back up my arguments."

Remove the emotional sting of events and personalities and their adverse affect on you, and you treat them in terms of context. It is another attitude that can help move your career forward.

#3: BETTER BUSINESS— CLIENT-CENTERED THINKING

What if you took the same attitude toward your boss and your company that you take toward your company's customers and clients? What do I mean? You probably go out of your way for customers or clients, stretching a bit, accommodating, listening intently, urgently wanting to make the sale or keep the sale.

Now. What if you changed your attitude, shifting from thinking of yourself strictly as an employee to seeing yourself as an in-house service provider? "Sounds complicated," one manager in a paper products company said. "Impossible when I tell you what the head of the men's department is like," a head buyer in men's furnishings for a large clothing store told me.

Both may be surprised at how simple the relationship can change and they can improve their status on the job. Here's how:

The client-provider relationship shifts responsibility for a successful mutual outcome on the shoulders of the whole team—including you. The client-provider mindset offers you a sense of equality that has never been available to you before as employee only. It encourages you to flex your entrepreneurial and intrapreneurial spirit. It allows your more opportunities for success. Only if you fail to satisfy the client do you fail.

The differences can sound something like this:

> **Employee:** "I was hired to do my job and I'm doing it."
> **Provider:** "Am I giving my client what he's paying for?"
>
> **Employee:** "This project is getting off track, but it's not my problem."
> **Provider:** "This project is off track and I have an idea of how to get it going in the right direction."
>
> **Employee:** "I don't get how to do this and no one is showing me how."

> **Provider:** "I need an expert advisor and think I know who I can call for a name. Or, if I learn how to do this, I could perform this service for my client."

In a focus on client-centered thinking, *Soundview Executive Summaries* said that power is on your side when you approach "top mangers like an autonomous outside contractor." They wrote that a client-provider relationship "opens your eyes to such things as: work flow efficiencies that keep you from becoming a low-cost supplier, slow cycle times that prevent you from being the first to market or deliver inventory in time, and conflicts between quality standards and productivity schedules."

You operate, to coin a phrase, like a virtual business. In today's marketplace, real outside providers compete with you to service the client, your company. You need to adopt the same attitude the competition is bringing to your company. (And while being indispensable is the ideal, you want to strive to be chosen, respected and liked, close enough to indispensable.)

When you think like a provider in a virtual business, an "outsourcing" attitude becomes second nature to you. Then it's easier to take the lead and meet a client's objectives and you're on the way to strengthening your "staying" power.

Here's why. If you were the boss, whom would you want to stay: someone who only does what's expected of him/her and shows little interest in helping the company grow, or a true team player who goes beyond "making a living," shows initiative and growth potential?

#4: BECOMING MORE CLIENT-CENTERED— WHAT TO DO NEXT

"How do I figure out what my boss wants? Where the company's going? How far I can step over the line and take up the role of provider?" people ask me all the time. How do you learn to see the client's needs, rather than work only to protect my own needs, and therefore, my job.

The client, your employer, looks at the broad picture. Your department, your position and the service you provide are only one small, though important, piece of the picture. To take advantage of a client/

provider focus and see what your employer does, you need to stand back and take in the view.

I think Kathleen Lingo's story tells it well here:

After a lengthy search, Kathleen was employed as the computer maven in a not-for-profit organization. Instead of simply reading the manual for her new job, she went one step further and asked her boss for specifics of why her predecessor didn't work out, so she wouldn't repeat his mistakes. She discovered the man's interpersonal skills were very poor and that he was known for never listening to anyone else. Kathleen's antenna went up. She told me:

> The first assignment I gave myself was to sit down with all the department heads and ask them for their computer wish list. Not that I needed to fulfill it all in the next six months or even a year. But I was at least giving them a chance to express what they wanted and showing them I was service-oriented, caring, and on their side.
>
> It was the first time those department heads were heard by the computer division!

At the same time that Kathleen was reshaping her relationship with the other departments, she took notice of who in her domain required extra attention: it was Nate*, the "tekkie" underling she'd inherited. Nate would make the department even more efficient—she needed his brain power harnessed and deputized to her.

The previous manager had put him in the role of a nerdy outsider who was easily replaceable. Kathleen saw more. She invited him for a posh lunch out at her own expense, wooed him, and made him feel important and part of the team. Of course, he produced for her and felt better about his own job.

An ability to see clearly what your client wants depends on your being able to see yourself clearly—what you do now and what you can do in the future. Not what you know, but what you can learn. Not what service you currently provide, but what service your client may need you to provide next week or next year.

Gain general knowledge of the business you're in. If you work in a dish factory, learn about the "tabletop" market, its trends, the competition, including imports, how your company advertises, gets its products in the magazines and papers. The more general knowledge you have of your company's structure, its culture, which employees up and down the line do what. The more you'll be able to assess and fill your client's needs or transfer your skills to another department. The wider your perspective, the easier it will be for you to judge where you can transfer.

Do you know your company's profit/loss statement looks like? Does your company have an annual report? Read it! It will give you general knowledge and allow you to communicate across departmental lines. At least superficially, your coming as an interested and thoughtful service provider can help you move up.

If you're in sales, don't just look at figures for the month, take a look at the department's achievement. How are you doing as a team?

If you're in customer service, pull up the orders for the last year of your two best customers. What did they buy? How long do they have to wait for their order? Can you help them in any way by providing an order in advance of need?

The more you know about your client—the company you work for—the more likely you are to provide what they need.

➤ Ask yourself how you view yourself vis-a-vis your organization. Do you consider yourself "just doing a job" to pick up your paycheck? Can you see yourself as a "service provider" and your company as "your client?"

➤ Can your department pay for itself or will they be going outside? Are you, as part of this department, saving them money? I asked a manager of a bank, how client-centering and outsourcing had changed her company? Nancy* told me:

> We used to have a big typing pool, now people either have their own computers, one assistant or, in a few cases, executives send work out to a service. Before we had a graphics department, now those jobs are mostly cut and we use desktop publishing/ graphic design programs. If there's anything else we need, it's outsourced—supplemented with temporary help.

➤ Think of how you would conduct yourself if you were a sub-contractor, a consultant or on a short-term contract assignment. If your current company was your highly coveted client, how would you delineate the service that you provide?

➤ Think about how you approach a customer on behalf of your company: You seek to give the customer what he wants, placate his discomfort, anticipate his needs, overlook his shortcomings. After all, he's paying for the product you sell.

#5: TEAMWORK AND TEAMS— THE NEW PLAYING FIELDS OF WORK

Studies of team systems on the job are part of the wave of the future and what you may well expect where you work. Probably with not a little influence from the work style of Japanese business, teams are just what they sound like—small or large groups of people working together on a product, service or procedure.

The team is responsible for the entire operation in one department or they can be "cross-functional"—just what they sound like. These interdepartmental teams are comprised of people from different departments who carry out different functions. Some teams are permanent and some are temporary, depending on the project, the product or the need.

It's a bit like football, a working unit of individual skills, agility and strengths working together to win, the coaches and owners on the sideline. Teams still allow for outstanding performance—the system is not meant to neutralize or deflate abilities and aspirations.

If there's any difference to get used to about teams—other than its soon to be commonality on the job—it would begin with the shift in leadership: There's usually no supervisor or "boss" as we'd recognize it. Rather, a more democratic process is in operation, wherein the team sets goals, monitors progress, hires others and may even buy equipment.

Teams may even decide to enter a "cross-training" program which allows them to rotate through a company, training up and down the supplier-customer chain—a program more typically applied in factories and manufacturing plants.

For a team to work smoothly within the company, each person must understand how things work and what's expected of them. Employers, then, provide coaches to help train workers in interpersonal skills, how to develop performance goals, dealing with customers and clients—all the primary requirements of success for the team.

"We're used to individual achievement," a hospital administrator with great aspirations commented to me about teams. "Am I supposed to think altruistically? Give up the ball, so to speak, to someone else for the good of the game? If so, I'm out! This will never really work for me."

Her consternation is not uncommon when the subject of teams comes up; teams sound especially cumbersome to hard-driving achievers. But is she expressing what many others think, too? Can teams fly in our manager-centered society where we're used to individual achievement, a designated leader and a chance to surpass that leader?

What happens when you're not quite ready to make the switch to teams?

Take the case of Steve Harrison*, a manager of a team at a Fortune 500 food company. In charge of 12 people that oversaw all aspects of production of five brands, Steve felt self-assured and sure-footed as he rose in the hierarchy. He was good with his manager although he was known as a man who bossed around the dozen people under him.

When the company decided to try the team system, they aimed for Steve's bailiwick. Top management reviewed output and profits and identified problems in four out of five of Steve's departments. They hoped that the team approach would improve output, profits and employee morale. Steve balked when he was "demoted" to team member, but with seniority. He said:

> The company wants the teams to change it, to make it
> richer and run better. I get that.
> What I don't get is why I'm suddenly working in a com-
> mune—they can call it what they like. I knocked myself out
> to get to this position, then the power is taken from me.
> What's in it for me if I help change this company? Where do
> I go? To the next chair over? I want to move up, not hold

hands with the guy next to me. We're not equals. Teams are a big management mistake.

Now what do I get?

Part of the company's instituting the team system in Steve's department was to increase those employees sense of participation and satisfaction. Only Steve hasn't adjusted. He knows what productivity should be, what the brand should do in the marketplace. He understands what was once his job, but not what the company wants of him now.

One of the most difficult problems with instituting the change to teams is that companies don't think out how to best use some of their supervisors and managers. These people are suddenly stripped of titles and/or authority and are made one spoke of the wheel.

The book, *Inside Teams*, by Richard S. Wellins, William C. Byham and George R. Dixon, followed the operation of teams in business and reported favorable results. They found that teams: invigorated a mature business, reported cost savings, increased production and showed priceless improvements in worker loyalty, motivation and enthusiasm.

Salaries and compensation, the authors also found, favorably corresponded to increased production. In fact, companies set up various types of pay scales, grading systems, bonuses, merit increases and profit-sharing incentives determined by team output.

Are teams best suited for smaller companies? Apparently not.

Companies like high-tech manufacturer Texas Instruments and food wholesalers and retailer Hannaford Brothers both reported good results, where the "work place structure pushes decision-making responsibility down to those doing the work." A former site manager, now part of a team said, "We started to notice that when people took ownership of results, good things started to happen." The authors of *Inside Teams* also quoted one less-satisfied manager who felt he'd lost his hard-earned role of "boss." He said, "It felt like the rug was being pulled out under me."

Where's your future in teams?

American business will continue to spotlight the stars, and the firmament may soon be spotlighting your name. But for most of us, business is changing and that means radical organizational shifts will increase the need for teams. The role of boss as we recognize it will disappear.

Therefore, the managers who remain will take on new roles of importance—they'll be used more as mentors, coaches or facilitators. As hierarchies continue to flatten and controls are replaced by trust, leaders will step out of functional slots and top management and recombine as teams.

Your company may not be trying out operational innovations on the order of teams quite yet, but there's a good chance that management is thinking how to improve profitability of your department. Another sort of teamwork. And what they're recommending is coaching.

Actual "team systems" cannot function unless members are coached in procedure, duties, attitudes, limits, required skill sets and more. Companies based on tiers or hierarchies—that is, most American companies now—also need employees with sharpened proficiencies and finer interpersonal skills and the people who can help make it so, or coaches.

#6: ADVISERS AND ALLIES—
HOOKING UP WITH MENTORS

What if you reach a career crossroads, restless to move up? You know you need to learn certain skills and want to get them from the best. Can you? Or, perhaps you're thinking, I'm 35, 40 or 50; am I too old for a mentor...would someone even consider me as a protégé? More adventuresome, you want to change careers and need the practical advice of an expert to point you in the right direction.

At mid-career you need an entirely different kind of adviser than you did when you started out. Back then, there was someone to help you figure out the basics, the rules, the game at hand. The "someone" was probably in a supervisory capacity, but the connection may not have had the personal touch—the "x-factor" in a mentoring relationship.

With a mentor, you find someone unique to champion you—someone who is a guide; someone who will impart her/his wisdom and understands that once you have developed, you may well surpass her/him. A mentor, technically, then, is a person who fulfills all or a combination of three main functions for you:

> ➤ a role model
> ➤ a promoter or sponsor of your career
> ➤ a counselor or adviser.

Before you make that call (or pen a note) to someone you've selected to be your mentor, be clear about what you're looking for. Ask yourself these two questions first:

➤ Is the person you think ideal for the role of your mentor in a politically advantageous position to help you? Are you really seeking connections into a job? A well-connected contact is not the same as a mentor.

➤ Second, what do you want to learn from your mentor? Are you sure that person can provide what you need? You may discover that you require more than one mentor from whom you can learn or observe. Finally, you can borrow the qualities from your mentor/s that work for you.

I recently spoke to a fascinating example of the mentor relationship—fascinating because the woman was a successful entrepreneur in her mid-40s when she decided to make a drastic change in her professional and personal life.

Cynthia Ciasulli Astrack, a dynamic, upbeat strawberry blond, closed her own company—where she was founder and president—and joined her husband's business in the summer of 1994 when she was 44. The switch signaled for her a complete change in industry, company size and to whom she was accountable.

Cynthia began C-COM, her consulting and marketing research company—where she specialized in telecommunications and high-tech products—after executive positions with DuPont, ITT and AT&T. She structured her company so she wouldn't have permanent employees on the payroll, just independent contractors she could rely on. This way, it could be large or small as the projects demanded—and she often ran three-to-five projects simultaneously.

After a few years of thinking about whether or not it would work, Cynthia said "yes" to her husband's proposal of joining him in his business. This meant a number of radical changes: She went from president and founder of her own company, to vice president of marketing at Astral Extracts, her husband, Alexander's, company. Her "product" changed from high-tech hardware to raw materials supplied to the flavor and fragrance industry. In her own business, she'd set her own methods of working; now she had to comply with her husband's working rhythms.

Of course, the big question is: Can spouses work together in accord—especially when one is learning the trade and the other is both mentor and "boss"?

I remembered a comment a friend made to me. Sharon wanted to join her husband's business, but Bob turned her down. Sharon said, "at first Bob worried that if I joined him, he'd be afraid to argue with me if I screwed up. Then when I asked him a few years later, he said no again. This time he was afraid that all we *would* do was argue!"

I asked Cynthia if she worried about disagreements on the job inherent in a mentoring relationship or treading on the more intimate husband-wife territory. Cynthia told me:

> No, it wasn't like Sharon's story for us.
>
> Alexander was always running a more successful company than mine. Years before I started C-COM, he thought I was being exploited by the big companies I worked for. Then when I went out on my own, he thought I was overworked!
>
> Basically, he always had it in his mind that I should work with him, but it took time for him to feel comfortable with the full reality of "do I bring my wife in with me?" I felt I couldn't miss an opportunity to learn a business like this from the top, which happened to belong to my husband.
>
> We set up very few boundaries, but we did decide on one rule: when we left the office we wouldn't talk about business, unless it was a critical problem. We held to that and I surprised myself that I could do it because I had a thousand questions.
>
> I also accepted that Alexander is the boss and if he made a decision I didn't agree with, I said, "He controls this company, he knows better and is teaching me while I learn."

I wondered how Cynthia's husband is a mentor and what he gives her that's different from what she's given herself, so to speak, as a former president of her own company. What kind of growth was there for her? She explained:

> Alexander is 20 percent role model and 80 percent adviser, but when I started out with him, it was the opposite. I

respect what he's done—starting this business from scratch, the great relationships with clients he's maintained. It gives me inspiration.

The skill sets I used at my own company—like great sales ability—my husband didn't need to train me in. But he's my mentor in guiding me in how to use that ability, and showing me what companies my personality will match best to, where to knock on doors and how to negotiate. You can spend one day listening to Alexander on the phone and learn how to handle any sort of person, anywhere in the world.

Alexander has everything in place, but I admit, I'd like to double the size of the company. This idea is fine with him, as long as it won't take time away from him on a personal level or enter or impose upon his work load.

Her husband is not Cynthia's first mentor. When she started at Du-Pont, as one of the first women executives in sales, a 63-year-old man with two years to retirement took her "under his wing," taught her how to dress, wear her hair, speak in public, handle meetings with executives at any level and completely molded her. And she succeeded at DuPont. She says:

I was lucky enough to be in the right place at the right time, and lucky enough to find such a great mentor and coach. And lucky it happened again!

The difference between mentor and coach walks a fine line, but the similarities can produce the same good results for you. As you'll discover, you don't have to think "football" to benefit from coaches:

#7: ADVISERS AND ALLIES— HONING SKILLS WITH COACHES

As hierarchies flatten and teamwork is becoming a reality, more and more companies are making the decision to coach employees, a kind of tougher training on the job. Coaches are hired, not only to get enthusiasm up, but to guide executives on how to manage, how to be more productive, how to work as a team.

If you think team sports, the realms of coachdom, you may get a picture of a barrel-chested guy with a whistle around his neck, hooting insults when a player trips, falls and is slow to bounce to his feet. Coaches, as we know, tend not to be interested in a player's opinion, he cares about results.

Part of a coach's ability to steer the team is his distance from the actual action—he not only knows the game, but he observes players, their skills, how they interact with others on the team, what their short-comings are, how to press their advantage.

Business is about profit and competition and so the sports meta-phor has found its way, in a moderate and refined manner, into in-dustry. The company coach, probably in a tailored suit and holding a file folder, is now on the payroll, determined to get better results from you by his more effective analysis of the work-situation and his instruction.

Who confronts a company coach? It could happen in one or both of two ways: You may be asked to describe the strong and weak points of the people you work with, ask how you perceive the job to be done and how you think others see you perform. Or, they'll ask people you work with what they think of your work, being specific. In this way, you get to understand what other people are saying about you while you can point out issues and give examples from co-workers.

Whether coaching is inevitable at your company or not, coaching—autodidactic or through a professional—implies growth. You need to ask yourself if you're someone who can be coached or is uncoachable, as with Vic Gray*, a customer service manager at a national discount chain store. Vic's the guy who knows all the answers, who never asks questions, has no interest in what others have to say, and is quick to tell you he's done it before and better.

Will Vic rise any higher than his overblown ego and narrowly-drawn formula of what makes a good manager? Probably not, unless he's will-ing to change.

And here's what happened: A coach came in and evaluated Vic, saw how he functioned on a multilevel team, made suggestions to him so he could be more productive, fit in and work in his best interest. Vic fought tooth and nail to have things remain his way. The company, though, at first, wanted Vic to stay—he had a gritty, if outdated, meth-od of getting things done. But they're a company in transition, having been purchased by a conglomerate. Since they're trying to blend everything together, Vic became the mongrel ingredient. The company had to let Vic go, simply for being uncoachable, and as he said to be, "too smart-assed for my own good."

Unlike Vic, some people find themselves not only coachable, but capable of becoming the coach.

Bonnie Maitlen, the independent consultant besides being an excellent trainer, has a gift for coaching and bringing others along in a seemingly effortless style. But there's a lot of depth in her technique. She told me about a more recent experience for her as a coach.

Bonnie had just been given full responsibility for recruiting, screening, identifying, certifying and training all Lee Hecht Harrison trainers nationwide. It was a big job, and Bonnie needed an associate who was on the ball and didn't need coddling. She hired Jill, whose experience was in mid-level management positions; in fact, they'd previously worked together at one of the companies. She said:

> When I brought Jill in, she didn't know anything about structure and I threw a lot of things at her quickly. I knew she could handle it because I've seen her cope before, and what she did was start to organize around what was "thrown" at her.
>
> In the beginning she was too shy and insecure to take the initiative and she waited for me to tell her what to do. She wanted to have me around a lot, but I'm on the road a great deal. She had to take charge—and she did.
>
> She created ways of organizing the work, she established relationships with the different offices and now people call and ask for her, rather than me.
>
> But she took advantage of the opportunity and didn't shy away from it.

What allowed a woman like Jill to grow from capable, timid worker to take-charge executive? How did Bonnie's coaching affect her so productively. She said:

> I think the biggest thing I gave her was permission to move. I also told her what I felt about her, that she knew as much about this as I did, that she was an excellent manager and that I trusted her judgment.

As to coaching, I told Jill to listen to me while I was interviewing and screening people and to follow my system. I didn't expect her to be perfect in the beginning, but I think my belief in her and my support allowed her to make a few mistakes and recover gracefully. Jill would say, "Gosh, I was awful on that one!" and I'd answer, "You didn't die over the mistake. Now tell me what you've learned from it." I could see how my help was valuable to her and it meant a lot to me, too.

What Bonnie did was what a coach must focus on: how to help others sort things out, find their own "greatness" and exercise their abilities with confidence.

George Haggerty, a New York consultant who puts franchise businesses together, has great insight about succeeding in business. He told me:

You have to ask yourself, how can I achieve greatness? You can be a great person—there's something for everybody—someplace where you can really be outstanding. But you have to find it and sometimes, you have to let someone help you find it.

A mentor, a coach, even the team itself, may bring out what you do best. What makes you a human being is you're not just one-dimensional—if all you're known for is how you grind out the numbers, then you will always make a good enough impression. But is that sufficient for you to have a fulfilling career?

WRAP-UP

➤ It's a fact that people plateau—who don't move up and stay in the same job—because there's no place, or fewer places, available for us to rise to. People at the top, in fact, may have plateaued, too.

➤ You can decide if you want your life to have no momentum or if you want to create new opportunities and redefine your goals.

➤ Only 1 percent of people are on the fast track and make newsworthy careers for themselves.

➤ When you hit a problem at work that seems overwhelming, instead of bemoaning the content of each issue—the report, the memo train, the impossible co-workers—objectify it. Distance yourself from what is bothering you and think in terms of context: how the greater issue fits into the scheme of things to help move productivity along. Taking the vicissitudes of the job subjectively binds you emotionally to unimportant issues.

➤ Take the same attitude toward your boss and your company that you take toward your company's customers, clients and suppliers. When you shift your focus from thinking of yourself solely as an employee to acting as if you are an "in-house service provider," you increase your sense of equality.

➤ When you become "client-centered," you are encouraged to be more entrepreneurial, allowing you more opportunities for growth and success within the company.

➤ Figure out what your boss wants and where the company is going, rather than work only to protect your own needs, therefore, your job.

➤ Be willing to seek guidance, coaching and find a mentor to help you learn what you need to know to get to the next level, apply your knowledge and get the support of someone who will be your career champion.

6

UNDERSTANDING WHO YOU ARE IN THE SCHEME OF THINGS

In the 1950s, author Ayn Rand caused a great stir with her book, *The Virtue of Selfishness.* In a time when company loyalty meant signing on and doing what you were told for 25 years or more so you could claim your pension, when being a dutiful child meant taking up the family business and marrying the person everyone thought was best for you, it was Rand's choice of words, not her message, that carried the bulk of her offense.

"Selfishness" was one of those emotionally-loaded words that suggested a lack of morality, like "greed" did in the 1980s. Selfishness sounded the spoiled kid who made demands, grabbed at what was not given, flaunted his own triumphs but scorned the success of others, and who always took the last piece of cake.

Selfishness also had a productive side, though it might be acknowledged begrudgingly: it implied a desire for self-determination which was driven by your own needs, not by what others wanted of you.

Self-determination was a principle we'd been taught was, if not profligate, then certainly anti-social, and anti-establishment. Selfishness implied that if we decided to grow and develop in a direction that rewarded our ambitions and talents, our real reward would be loneliness, even within monumental success. Like Howard Hughes, we may change an industry and gain riches, but as a consequence, the "self" would deteriorate, become insular, estranged from the real world.

Rand's actual definition of what constituted selfishness was, in fact, laudable! The basis of her message was simple: If each of us set our goals and carried them out, society would be the better for it. Hardly an undermining radical idea!

If anything, this kind of professional selfishness—knowing yourself and what path you can take in the work place—is the foundation to remaining employable. "I agree with that idea, yet I don't," Francine Pauly*, a hospital administrator specializing in negotiations between union and labor, told me. She said:

> I remember that "do your own thing" ideal of the '60s, '70s and even the '80s set lots of people at sea. "Do your own thing" can be very vague and it doesn't mean, live by improvising.
>
> Now people need guidance to help them clarify what's best for them. I find people are little embarrassed when they're 30 or even 40 and still don't know what they want from a job and where their best chances can be found.

The mission to look inward can be a noble one. Of course, the real point of looking inward is to help you "do your own thing" while not turning the quest into your occupation. Ideally, you use what you've learned about yourself to function in the real world!

There's everything right about seeking self-knowledge so we can get more out of our jobs and, therefore, out of our lives, but let me add this important point. It's not enough to pursue activities to simply please and gratify yourself. You need to be aware of where you are so you don't lose some of your ability to read the environment and adapt yourself to it.

The people who'll thrive in their work, at their jobs and guarantee their own employability, are the ones who "see" what's going on around them and act.

What makes a "seeing" person? We have to go back to purposeful selfishness and pinpoint what kind of person you are in the work place, and where you can best function. This involves understanding how you take risks, deciding if you are a Finder or a Minder and if you are more productive in a small or a large corporation. Let's start here:

WHAT EVERYONE SHOULD KNOW ABOUT RISK TAKING

Experts in the field of human behavior have identified three basic types of risk takers, which I've renamed: risk junkies, cautious risk takers and educated risk takers. See where you fit:

➤ **The risk junkie:** You sometimes tend to be impulsive and move without first getting all the facts. You're optimistic and assume that there will be water in the pool because it has usually been there when you jumped off in the past! You love the thrill of the chance—the follow-through is less important.

   Marshall is an extreme example of the thrill addict. He needs to feel like a success, or in his terms, "an operator," so he's got eight or 10 balls in the air. These are deals he's trying to get into or, because he can't say no or appear as if he's made a mistake, deals he can't get out of. Some of his deals come through, if only because the odds go his way once in a while, but most of them fall through.

   "I can't pass up a scheme," Marshall said. "People are always calling me. 'Put me together with this guy,' they say, or 'Who do you know in Canada who could finance this deal?' This is how I do business. I couldn't depend on my job itself to support me, so I look for the angles. If I lose, there's always another call coming."

   If you have a little bit of Marshall in you, you're the biggest gambler of the three types. Your up side is that by being an opportunist and jumping on a possibility, you are actually there first and can strike gold when the odds are with you. Your down side is that you often don't consider the consequences of your action on others. Your family may suffer from your leaps of interest and you can lose credibility in the business world.

   It's not that you're trying to hurt people, but you have many leaps of interest and if you don't put some brakes on, you can lose credibility.

➤ **The cautious risk taker:** Decisions are painful because you're equally worried about success and failure. You may even deny there's a full pool—an opportunity overflowing with possibility just inches from your foot. You eventually make a choice once you feel the outcome is sure. You are like Janet:

Janet Holm*, who's attractive and exceptionally smart, is nearing 30, and about to celebrate her eighth year of employment as assistant to the owner of a country club in south Florida. Wanting better for herself, Janet took courses at night at a nearby university, and got a master's degree in business, specializing in marketing. But she is stuck at her desk, billing golfers and organizing dinners, since she turned down a good job offer that would have taken her north, to Orlando.

"It just wasn't exactly right," Janet said. "None of the jobs I apply for sound worth my relocating. At least I have a job here—even though everyone says I can't go any higher unless I buy the place. I'm bored most of the day, but I can't seem to get myself to say yes and leave."

If you're like Janet, you may get stuck in the sense of security and familiarity at work, and find excuses not to excel. On your up side, you are the most thoughtful and deliberate of the risk takers, and are responsible, capable, though not much of a gambler. On your down side, a lack of faith in your ability keeps you stuck and frustrated in jobs that don't allow you to shine.

➤ **The educated risk taker**. You have vision and are not afraid to take a chance, but unlike the risk junkie, you do your homework first. You check out the possibilities and the probabilities, do the research and make the calls to give you a foundation. You approach the pool, so to speak, knowing the temperature of the water, how deep it is, and how to get across and back using the most efficient stroke. You only take risks where you feel the timing is with you and you are more than 75 percent sure of getting what you want.

Stan Lewis* is perfect here. Stan was working in an upper management job for a utility company, and eager to switch to a small manufacturing or service-oriented company—that is, he sought a profit-making company that manufactured or distributed products that interested him. A place where he could earn equity. He had to job hunt discretely, and through an uncle living in Texas, he learned of a two-year-old company, small but growing fast, that could use his talents.

Stan did his homework, checking on every aspect of its financing; since the company hadn't gone public yet, he couldn't get an annual report, but his uncle used his contacts to find out, in general, how solvent they were. Stan interviewed with the CEO and asked to see the offices, the plant, and asked the right questions about what the company wanted for itself.

"When I knew this job could change my life for the better," Stan said, "I told my wife I wanted to make the move from Michigan to Texas. At first, it bothered her, leaving home, her job, her family, but both of us knew that we'd have to take this chance."

If you're an educated risk taker, you've weighed both sides.

"In the New Economy, work is intensely personal. Because it has to do first with ideas and knowledge, rather than products and services, work begins with the self. It is a fusion of intuition and experience, informed less by the gathering of immutable facts than by decoding of mercurial patterns."

KLAUS SCHWAB AND CLAUDE SMADJA,
Harvard Business Review

THE FINDER

Economist John Kenneth Galbraith said, "Faced with the choice between changing one's mind and proving that there is no need to do so, almost everybody gets busy on the proof." Those not working on "the proof" are probably the Finders among us—people more interested in being innovative than redoing what's been done and mulling over the past.

What, then, will make you a Finder?

➤ Though you're certainly capable of changing your mind, and putting up a good argument, a Finder's catchword is progress. You like moving forward, going on to the next project and discovering new territories, hence your name. The Finder brings in ideas, and is always creating something—whether he/she works in a company, or with a company as a consultant, or, independently, as an entrepreneur or intrapreneur.

➤ Finders always survive because they bring in new sources of business while the Minders, to whom they delegate, get the work out. Finders want to become partners in a smaller company, or rise to president or CEO of a larger one, and everything they say or do affirms it.

I spoke to Renee Lerche, manager of education and planning, at Ford Motors in Detroit, who is a quintessential company-oriented Finder. She told she likes to "look ahead" even though she sees a ceiling in the distance. Still, Renee is a Finder. She said:

> "I'm going to stay because I'm too visible to fail. I can be in the top 150, but not chairman of this company. There are no women in the pipeline for CEO and only 27 women in the top 1000. The good news is that I will be promoted, the bad news is that I can't be CEO."

➤ Finders operate within a wide range of interpersonal skills, ranging from charismatic to questionable. Many Finders are so focused on a goal, that can they tread on others feelings on the way up and not realize it.

➤ Finders are instinctual "rainmakers"—they make things happen and bring in clients and business, even miracles, on occasion. Rainmakers can build strong relationships with customers and clients, ensuring the company's bottom line.

➤ A Finder may look around his work place one day and say to himself, "I can leave this office tomorrow and have a clientele that would go with me. All those people trust me!" If the circumstances demand it, Finders have the confidence to leave and get a better position. The more entrepreneurial Finder would start his own company.

➤ Some Finders hit a plateau and spelunk every possibility searching for the next step up the mountain. New Yorker Barbara Goodstein, a very engaging, enthusiastic woman and classic Finder, has reached such a toehold in her career.

Barbara's first job after school was at Warner Lambert, which she left because there was "no woman at the top," a concern she shares with Renee, at Ford. When she quit Warner Lambert, she was friendly with the then president of the company who couldn't understand why she'd leave.

"There are no women at the top," Barbara said to him, "and things won't change in five years or even 10 years." He assured her that a woman could rise at Warner Lambert and Barbara said, "not even in 15 years. That's how they do business, and women are not included."

Ten years later she is still right—no woman has moved into very top management.

Barbara's career from there took her to a number of large corporations, where she rose to vice president. Then at 34 years old, she quit her job at Banker's Trust to figure out where her real work lay. She didn't want to stay in a large corporation for any extended amount of time because she'd "gotten whatever learning" she can "get out of them." She told me how she felt:

> The next step I could aspire to in a large corporation would be a higher and higher position. But I watched women around me unable to rise, to be minimized and have authority taken from them. I don't want that to happen to me!
>
> So I'm trying to be proactive. I realize there's no long-term future for a woman within the next 10 years to run a large corporation, where I want to be, so I have to figure out something else to do. And that may be to start my own business.

Barbara's using her network of contacts to meet with people she can bounce ideas off of and get their feedback. She's talked to recruiters, analysts, potential mentors, women in business, and she is still doing exploratories. Within those two days she allots herself, she meets with people all day.

In the process of goal-setting, Barbara, needs to come to a conclusion about her direction and plan the strategy to move her there. She's giving herself one year's time to come up with the answer to her own question—where do I want to go? Each day, the picture clarifies a little more for her—and it looks like she may become an entrepreneur.

On the up side, Barbara has a tremendous capacity to understand what goes into making a decision—how to synthesize the information she's receiving from so many different angles.

To a Finder like Barbara, the down side of her one-year search is...

> I haven't done it yet and feel demoralized. I should have a business up and running!
>
> Of course, the safer route is to keep working for a company forever. I know I'm going to keep working, but for myself. In fact, when I left Banker's Trust, I told the person I freelance for now that I'm only going to work for one or two people ever again, myself or him. That's it.
>
> I feel I should take my chances.

> ➤ Finders often have a strong inclination for entrepreneurial or intrapreneurial endeavors. Intrapreneurship is about running a company that is a profit center of its own within another larger company.
>
> Rising in a corporation defines a Finder one way, founding a company is another. Could you stand the heat of being an entrepreneur?
>
> Starting, owning and running your own business requires a few qualities beyond the daily scope of even the most ambitious 9-to-5 "company man." The toughest element is raising start-up money to keep you afloat while you build a clientele and a reputation. After that, the successful entrepreneur must:
>
> > ➤ Be willing to work long and hard hours. You answer only to your own efforts and responsibility to the

business. Don't expect to start work at 9 or close shop at 5.

➤ Be emotionally able to manage the ups and downs of a small business and cope with extremes without giving up.

➤ Be able to handle rejection and bounce back with authority. New businesses are prone to be passed over since they haven't quite proven themselves in the market yet.

➤ Be realistic about your product or your service, and its potential in the marketplace.

In relation to entrepreneurial Finders, I heard a wonderful story about how three mid-managers who worked at the Marriott Hotel changed their fortunes. They were young and ambitious—25, 26 and 27 years old—and each evaluated the results of the downsizing at the hotel and compared notes. The all concluded that because of the dearth of supervision in the food and restaurant area, "a lot of people were cheating the company," Dan Moore, one of these ex-managers told me.

"It's very easy for cash to come across the bar and not be accounted for," he added. Dan and his two colleagues saw how they could improve the system and the profits for the hotel by outsourcing to the company: They quit their jobs and opened their own company. In six months they had 14 employees—and their major client was Marriott.

What do these guys do? They opened a "shopping service" wherein, posing as "customers," they come in to a restaurant and knowing what to look for, report on what they see. "We found that in 68 percent of the time, there's something going on," he said. As brilliant outsourcers, they've also put together a hotel training program for women that is paid for by suppliers to the hotel business, like the companies who supply tableware or bread.

This young Finder group has just put together their first conference, in which they invited the president of the Marriott and invited speakers and suppliers. Their new business is an ideal outsourcer— they know the "insiders" and they're filling the needs of the customers they know best.

The Staff Job vs. the Line Job: What's Right For You:

Who's who in the work place? Can a staff or a line job make the difference in terms of your future with a company?

➤ Staff jobs draw their strength from auditing, promoting, policing and acting as a conscience and form a kind of auxiliary function. Line jobs are involved with inventing, producing, marketing, selling, designing and delivering the product or service.

➤ Staff functions fulfill the support needs of a company and specialized areas of expertise such as finance, information systems, human resources, planning and legal. They're all there to assist the line in getting its product out.

➤ The first people to be downsized tend to have staff jobs. Fire the lawyers? Sure, a legal department is considered dispensable, since the company can always outsource— call in lawyers on contract, when they're needed.

➤ If you're a staff person in this marketplace, start thinking of yourself differently and sell your services in a smarter way. Think about how you can help the line do more than you did before. Give your company a service guarantee so you have don't have to compete with other outsource groups. How would you service your own employer so you don't have to worry about other outsourcers?

MINDERS

While many of us dream of leading, winning, of page-one triumphs, of six-and seven-figure incomes, there are those who are equally content to be part of a much needed support system and do not have any interest in reinventing the wheel. Most of the work force, in fact, belongs to this latter category.

Human beings are almost infinitely adaptable, will respond to circumstances and transform themselves over time into what they need to be. The fact of the matter is that many of us change and adapt just enough in terms of work for one very good purpose: The demand in our society calls for more people, who only want to do what they're told and who only want to follow orders.

If everyone were a leader or an entrepreneur in a company of any size, there would be chaos! There has to be a greater percentage of people who'll do the work or the world would grind to a standstill.

So while being a Finder may have its flash and life-changing glamour, being a Minder has depth, beauty, craftsmanship and dignity. Not a bad place to be.

What, specifically, then, makes you a Minder?

➤ Minders usually don't work for themselves since they prefer to hitch themselves to a star—and function at exceptional levels as the star's satellite. Minders like being number-two or two thousand—in the support position.

➤ Minders tend to insure their employability because they are most sensitive to what's happening around them and most capable of figuring out how to benefit themselves—and their bosses.

That is, Minders are good at reading the signs around them and never stop working. Even at a cocktail party. If someone gives a Minder a business card, the Minder will think over what this person does and where he works and decide how this new contact can help his boss and the company. He'd say, "I just met someone who works for a different phone company than the one we use and he has a plan that can help us reduce our monthly international calling charges."

➤ Minders can maneuver themselves into positions with an important title and a six-figure salary. But most Minders, because they stay in some level of middle management, earn mid-level salaries.

➤ Minders tend not to become partners in a small company, and in fact, probably don't want the title or the responsibility. To the Minder, the best thing about being a well-paid middle manager is that you do your work and go home and have your life.

➤ Minders have a quality of temperament that can keep them working in corporations at a mid- or upper support level: they don't challenge authority too dramatically. "I honestly think that a middle manager is a yes person, unless they're more of a maverick," said Don Carson*, a paralegal supervisor at a small law firm specializing in personal injury cases. "You're more concerned about keeping your job than telling anyone above you they're wrong. I hate to admit it, but that could be me."

➤ In keeping with the temperamental characteristics, Barbara Goodstein, who I introduced in Finders, offered a fascinating portrait of the Minder. She contrasted her work style and temperament with that of her husband, Bob. The comparison was meaningful because Bob is a version of the more dynamic Minder. She told me:

My husband will survive in a corporation forever. He's grateful for what they give him and he somehow knows what and where the line is and how he can make his point, but he doesn't cross that line.

He might keep rising slowly because when he doesn't rise fast enough he doesn't get mad at anyone. He protests, but all within moderation. But he doesn't protest enough to get them mad at him, either.

He's complaining at work now because I'm making him complain about not being promoted. Since he met me—that's four years—he's been promoted eight times. Before me, he'd been promoted once in five years!

Barbara adds that Bob has the "perfect combination" of qualities to be successful in a large corporation. She described them this way:

He's very intelligent and he's got me harassing him, but he's still so nice and obliging a person that all the objections that even sound aggressive or griping coming from him are acceptable.

I think that any person, who is actually incredibly intelligent like my husband, moderate in disposition, patient, and willing to live with less than perfection and bonuses that are reasonable but not outstanding will ultimately become very successful.

➤ Minders can find satisfaction as a support system to a boss, a department, or the profit-making machine of the company, but a Minder can also be a bureaucrat. You don't have to work for a government office or a utility company—the ultimate order of a bureaucracy—to be a bureaucrat.

Many very large corporations set themselves up to function by very strict interdepartmental rules, strict codes of behavior, greater reverence to the time clock, too many levels of paperwork to sign off on— the very nature of bureaucracy.

Many Minders thrive in the red tape of this system as happy managerial bureaucrats. These Minders tend to define themselves in terms of the appearance of power, and the appearance of power is measured by the number of people they have working for them and the size of their budget. To preserve their sense of identity, they have to preserve these areas of their reach. So they spend their efforts furthering that aim, and have to remind themselves not to lose sight of what the organization is about.

Futurist Arnold Brown had some thoughts on bureaucracy and those who function well within them. His own experience helped him draw his conclusion. He said: "Never underestimate the power of a bureaucracy to protect and preserve itself. My experience in bureaucratic organizations was that at least 50 percent or more of time and effort were spent on internal politics."

A friend of mine who teaches in college—another sort of bureaucracy—said that, "The reason academic politics have the reputation of being so nasty is because the stakes are so low. The stakes in academia are just intellectual primacy—which is a low stake in the business world."

Of course real smarts count in industry, but business places greater value on the ability to think on your feet, demonstrate shrewdness, understand the basics of negotiating a deal, get along with others, and the ability to problem solve as each day presents a different problem. The best qualities of the Minder.

Although people are more one type than the other in how they earn a living and find satisfaction in work, it's very possible to find subtle combinations of both. A Finder may be a Finder for himself but devote time, perhaps as a mentor, to be a support, or a Minder, to others. In turn, a Minder can be more comfortable in a support position, but be an aggressive or determined Finder for someone he cares about.

In today's environment you'll probably find yourself in both positions for a portion of your career—you're going to be a Finder and a Minder.

In celebration of 100 years of Labor Day—September 1994—Tom McNichol and Nadine Slimak in *USA Weekend* compiled a list of "dueling factions"—types, so to speak—that may be typically found in any company, large or small:

➤ Loyalists vs. job jumpers.

➤ In-office workers vs. telecommuters.

➤ Flextime vs. 9-5.

➤ Civil libertarians vs. drug test supporters.

➤ Working parents vs. "child free."

➤ Those who can unjam the copier vs. the technically challenged.

WHAT SUITS YOU BEST— THE LARGE OR SMALL COMPANY

"The fact of the matter is that life is better in a small corporation," Jeff Edwards*, the vice president of a small, successful mail order house told me, certain of his position. "Everyone in a small organization has a better shot at earning more or getting promoted faster. People feel like they belong someplace."

"I would perish in a small company," George Clark*, the editor of numerous in-house newsletters in a brand-name, huge corporation, asserted. "You're too limited in too many ways. This company is so large, I have choices. And if I want to leave, my experience here plus the name of the company itself opens doors."

There probably is little argument over whether you are more a Finder than a Minder, or perhaps a bit of both. But when it comes to where to ply your trade, company size always enters into the criteria for "the better place to work" and almost always stirs debate.

Jeff, the mail order house executive, believes that he can always anticipate greater rewards because a small organization will both notice and value him. Not lost in a great population of competitors, he's closer to the top.

George, the brand-name corporate editor, disagrees, seeing greater rewards in other benefits of size—access to a greater breadth of internal contacts, greater access to other skills in other departments, and a shot at the top—albeit a long shot. "You're not likely to get as much," he said. "Too many people want the sole spot on the top and the competition is very intense and probably even nasty in a large corporation. But small companies are claustrophobic, too much into everyone's pocket. Large is better for all its faults."

Look at it this way, too. If you were a Finder, your gifts of being an enterprising, gutsy, go-for-the-sale type would probably pay off higher dividends for you in a smaller company. The smart boss of a such a company wants to reward the talent that signs up business. If you bring in an account, you have more leverage if you say, "Look...20 percent commission isn't good enough anymore. XYZ Associates is a million dollar a year account. Now I want 40 percent of business I bring in." And you can negotiate from there with greater success.

Then again, if you're very adaptable, like Cynthia Ciasulli Astrack, who joined her husband in his business, and who was described in the previous chapter, the large company can prepare you for any eventuality. Cynthia said:

> Working at DuPont and AT&T plunged me into business and industry on a huge scale. My bosses there taught me the subtleties of business and surviving big company politics.
>
> I think that if you keep your eyes open, you can pick up from the successful people what you need to know and bring it anywhere.

Having operated a small marketing research company, Hyatt Esserman for 20 years, and before that, having worked for CBS, a huge television network, I can say I've been on both sides and identify with what each has to offer. I have a feeling that Cynthia, and people like her, wouldn't have had as smooth a transition to her latest venture had she not gone the gamut from a large corporation, to her own company, and finally, to an established small concern.

I put the question to Ernan Roman, president of a direct marketing corporation with clients in the Fortune 25 companies. Ernan had an interesting take on the difference between company size. Before opening his own firm, Ernan worked in a number of Fortune 500 large companies, and watched their structure and *modus operandi* change. He told me:

> In the last five years, I've seen a shift in large companies from a pride in innovation to a much more cautious, conservative approach.
>
> In a large company, there's always going to be bureaucracy, which I think is a function of its size and mass. Because of that mass, there has to be a social order to hold it together. An internal cultural norm. What happens when you get that order is the risk of conformity and uniformity. Then, many large companies, who've been on a long roll of success, have suddenly been hit and bloodied by the marketplace.

The changes in companies Ernan mentioned leave us with a lesson. They demand that you learn a degree of political acumen, sensitivity and patience so as to generate personal success in a large company— qualities demanded to a greater extent now than five years ago. You must be a champion of your career and a politically and personally astute player because in today's job sweepstakes, he says, "it's a make or break issue."

Okay, we know this: Marketplace economics have changed large companies and affected us all—half of America's companies were restructured in the 1980s and several hundred thousand were downsized. Even the notable giants cannot offer a guarantee of "lifetime employability," golden benefits and generous perks anymore. And chances are, you have to be a star at adaptability to make it to the top of a large organization.

Does this mean you should avoid the giants? Not at all! People still love the idea of a large, prominent and multifaceted organization—which still has the resources to grow—and nothing deters them from seeking a fulfilling career at the larger companies.

Many of the people I spoke to, who opted for large companies, enjoyed the variety and scope in products and co-workers' skill sets they found there. Some of these people have left or were edged out; others are still at a "megalith," and may make it to the day they collect a pension. But, I found, they're not interested in working at a particular company until retirement just to show they can hold on, but because they care to make the company better, not just sustain it.

However, when large companies are retrenched and people leave, many take up work at a smaller company. As futurist Arnold Brown said, "the more you try things, the more you're able." And this includes adaptability to a small company, it culture and its opportunities.

As Jeff Edwards, the vice president of the small mail order house, put it, "if you're smart in a small company, it has to pay off. You're appreciated." Not every small company operates with a culture of benevolence and equal opportunity, but your chances are better of being closer to senior management and the top—hence, you are noticed more often and your worth, noted. Added to that, there's a shorter path for action to be taken and making change as your span of control increases.

In a small company, said Jeff:

> You can get more out of people than they want to give. When the staff is small, you must wear many hats and be ready to jump in or take over. Because of that, you learn more, and your potential is greater. Sometimes, there's even magic.

Peggy Daniels, an enterprising and creative TV producer, talked to me about the "magic" that can come with a small company—and what she missed when the company grew, and she "grew up."

The company Peggy was referring to was WNET, the PBS station in New York City. It was 1963, and it had just gone on the air, offering a whole new concept in alternative television. It was also Peggy's first job, and it spoiled her. She told me:

I had no idea that the work world would be different any-where else. People at the station were intense, conscious they were doing something groundbreaking and it seemed important to us.

We were paid low salaries but given a great deal of latitude to do anything we wanted. There was a feeling that we were in it together, creating something new. The whole world was looking at us. It created a bond between the people I knew in those days.

It's not that we all necessarily remained friends in a social sense, but even now there's always a welcome contact made.

After a number of years, Peggy worked in the production end, freelancing under contract on a show or a series. If the series was canceled or finished its run, she'd get upset. To her it meant she would "go away and they'd still be there." The station to her was "family," only under contract, she said:

I felt like an outsider, where I was no longer in the tight family circle, because I had to leave when my job was over. But they were always there for me to go back to.

Then I grew up. I found that there were plenty of other companies to work for where there were great people. But more importantly, I accepted the fact that I was a freelancer or an ad hoc person and that it had a good aspect to it.

I didn't necessarily want a full-time position with a happy family sort of company. I just wanted things that went along with it—a paycheck, security, health benefits.

But the most important quality the station gave to Peggy before it grew from 60 to 600 employees, was the "bonding with the people at the station—so much more than a working situation."

FINALLY

While you must be able to define yourself to best sell yourself in this marketplace, also know that you are not your job title or, in fact, only one type. There are phases in your career when you are a Minder, but circumstances change, you adapt, and emerge a Finder. The point is to get a grasp on how you best function, learn to read the signs well around you and synthesize your experiences, your interests, your vision for yourself and your goals—the focus of the next chapter.

WRAP-UP

➤ Be aware of what's happening in the work place. Sharpen your ability to read the environment and adapt yourself to it. People who thrive on the job and guarantee their own employability are the ones who "see" what's going on around them, and act.

➤ Could you be an entrepreneur? Be sure you are you emotionally equipped to handle the roller coaster ride that every start up goes through.

➤ Know what kind of risk taker you are:

The risk junkie tends to be optimistic, impulsive, loves the thrill of chance—and moves without first getting all the facts. You love winning. The cautious risk taker is equally worried about success and failure, therefore slow to make a decision. You eventually make a choice once the outcome seems assured. The educated risk taker has vision and is not afraid to take a chance, but unlike the risk junkie, you do your homework first.

➤ What type are you in the work place—a Finder or a Minder?

The Finder's catchword is progress—going on to the next project, discovering new territories, bringing in ideas and always creating something—whether they work in a company, with a company as a consultant, or, independently.

Minders prefer to hitch themselves to a star and like being in a support position. They tend to insure their employability by being sensitive to what's happening around them and figuring out how to benefit themselves— and their bosses.

➤ Company size affects how fast you will rise and how much you will earn. Generally, you can anticipate greater rewards in a small organization that will both notice and value you. Since you're not lost in a great population of competitors, you're closer to the top.

There can be a benefit to size—larger companies give you access to a greater number of contacts, allow for mobility to other departments or company branches, good salaries, some perks (most companies across the board have cut these), and even a shot at the top.

7

MISSIONS, GOALS AND EVERYTHING YOU NEED TO KNOW ABOUT ORGANIZING YOUR CAREER

"**W**here do you see yourself in five years?"

It's a familiar if sometimes puzzling interview question, one we've all confronted. You may respond with, "I can't think five years into future. I want this job now—let's see about five years down the line when five years are up!" You may hesitate to say what you're thinking to the person on the opposite side of the desk— the person who might well be your boss tomorrow: "Okay. In five years, I see myself sitting in this office and I hope to have your job!"

The question may sound almost irrelevant in today's job-hopping marketplace, but it actually addresses an issue as critical to good business as it ever was: What do our employees want for themselves and will they find it in our company? Your response to the question is really one way for them to gauge your goals and your vision—what you want now and what you project for yourself into the future.

"How does knowing my five-year plan affect a company?" people ask me. "I work for them; they're in business to make a profit, not to make me happy! I can only succeed there if they run the company so it grows and can accommodate my growth."

On the contrary, the entity known as "the company" is first made of people, who structured a business, sell some sort of product and operate out of an edifice, great or small. To exist into the next century, knowing your goals works to its advantage.

In the *Harvard Business Review*, authors Robert and Judith Waterman and Betsy Collard suggest that mutual interest in reaching goals represent a new covenant between American workers and their employers, in which, they write, "both share the responsibility for maintaining the individual's employability inside and outside the company."

This ideal almost implies an even exchange in which the employee pledges his commitment to the company and the community in exchange for supplemented and maximized employability with a company who knows who he is and where he wants to go.

"It's the employee's responsibility to manage his or her own career," Waterman and Collard wrote in the *Review.* "It is the company's responsibility to provide employees with the tools, the open environment, and the opportunities for assessing and developing their skills."

So back to basics:

When hiring personnel or determining who should stay and who should go in a downsizing, managers look to keep those who are self-motivated, who have professional vision and who work hard to not only get the job done, but to further their personal goals, as well. Experts have found that people with personal and professional goals are more creative, attempt more problem-solving tasks, and continually seek to increase and enhance their skills.

So in this chapter, I want to offer seven key satellite issues for you to look at in terms of achieving your goals. They are: defining your mission, goal setting, understanding competition, becoming visible, tooting your own horn, asking for what you want and networking.

Take this opportunity now to assess your skills and career objectives. Let's begin with your mission.

DEFINING YOUR MISSION

Every successful career has a mission, that one broad vision that defines the direction you want your career to take. If you look back on every job you've ever had—even if on the surface it does not appear to be a logical continuum—you will find an underlying thread that connects one to the other.

In each position you may have held different titles and used varying skills, but the basic underpinnings are the same. You and your value system, the ways you want to participate, will be strikingly similar.

Some people are defined by their mission, and for them, a career path is less a choice than destiny. The great dancer, Martha Graham, was 19 before she took a single dance lesson, inspired to learn and perform after seeing Ruth St. Denis on stage.

Other people you and I would know, people with a "gift" of some sort may also be struck by an inspirational example or simple internal knowledge: "I knew I wanted to be an architect when I was four years old. There was never anything else..." "My father took me to visit his uncle, a doctor, in Salt Lake City when I was six years old. The moment I met him, I knew there'd be no other life for me but medicine..." "I love sewing, making clothes. My mother says handiwork is in our blood. I even have a fragment of a quilt made by my great-grandmother."

Most of us, though, must either be inspired by, or find our way through, the astonishing possibilities of careers and occupations that the 1990s makes available.

What do you want to accomplish? Fulfilling your mission makes work worthwhile and gives you the chance to make a difference in your world.

You must know your mission so that you can build objectives, set goals and get out there! If you don't have a focus, you'll be standing on the dock all your life, watching others sail off, wondering what's out there—and what you missed out on.

In looking for your mission and setting your objectives and goals, it's important to consider all the alternatives, pick up every rock. Keeping your focus broad when you start out allows you to clarify what you want and in which direction you should go. When you come to a conclusion, be prepared, if necessary, to throw it all out and start over.

"If you don't know where you're going, any path will lead you there," someone said very wisely. Find your mission, then...

STATE YOUR GOAL

To maintain your lifetime employability, understand that everything that goes on around you in business can influence your future. Every meeting, every networking opportunity, every day you work, there exist opportunities to secure information to help you set new goals or adjust old ones.

"I see myself in the corner office," a 30-year-old woman said, at one of my workshops. "I watch how the current vice president handles herself and I know I could do her job better. How can I prove it?"

"I want to quit my job and work on a small town newspaper in the west," a young man working as a tax accountant told me. "I didn't go to journalism school; friends say no one would hire me without experience. I'm a born reporter."

"I know I'm the best salesman in my company," a young man I met at a sales seminar told me. "I want to win the company's trophy for best sales record this year, but my customers aren't buying and I'm $25,000 off the mark."

Before you can state your goal, you need to be aware of what you're capable of and what's possible within the context of your present career situation.

What innate knowledge do you possess that will help you reach your goal? What credential or track record do you have that demonstrates your ability to achieve it? What avenues are available in your company to help you accomplish your goal? Is your goal realistic?

Goals should be:

➤ specific.

➤ achievable.

➤ consistent with your personal life plan.

Big goals with large numbers sound good, but you must have a reasonable and do-able plan to get you what you want. People are often overwhelmed by what seems like the enormity of a goal once they put that goal to paper.

One sure way to meet a goal is by establishing deadlines for short-term achievements—that is, to think big, first think small. This makes perfect sense. By breaking down your goal into smaller pieces, you focus on the specific steps you need to take and in what manner. Think strategy, target and objective. These points lets you move forward.

Let's take John Wills*, the salesman who's $25,000 short of a best sales record. John's go to sell that amount of his product in 14 days to achieve his immediate objective, raise his commission base and get a bonus and a promotion, his ultimate goal. His solution:

John set a daily goal: 20 cold calls a day.

He set a weekly goal: Contact 10 inactive clients in person and 20 active clients in person.

He created summarized marketing materials to support his efforts and made it easier for him to target a particular client.

Result: At the end of two weeks, John not only succeeded in making his mark, but exceeding it by another $10,000.

Six Tips to Help You Figure Out Your Goal

1. Be aware of what's happening in the industry of your choice and what's possible for you.
2. Scrutinize your credentials to find the connections and skills sets that can be applied to achieving your goal. Don't underestimate your abilities.
3. Make your own luck! It's not just others who always seem to be in the right place or the right time. If you hear about an opportunity, seek it out. Don't let anyone talk you out of taking a "lucky" chance.
4. Let other people know what your goals are. Silence, secrecy, modesty and contemplation are the missions of monks, not people in business. Discuss your goals with others, who may well bring you the break you seek.
5. When you define your goal, set down the steps you can take to support it. Your goal need not be company- or industry-specific, but it should include a direction from which you can construct a career map.
6. Join professional associations, learn more about your field, or, if you want to change fields, network with others who can introduce you to another industry.

KEEP YOUR GOALS REALISTIC

Whatever your interim goals, they can be attainable if you are willing to do three things:

➤ remain flexible about how to achieve goals.

➤ review your goals periodically in light of new information.

➤ make sure your goals don't conflict with the mission of the goals of your employer, clients or customers.

Remember, achieving your goals has an effect on others, too. If you're working in an organization, your goals have to stay in sync with everyone else's, no matter what mission you are pursuing. In order to be in sync, communicate with higher-ups around you, and make yourself aware of your company's mission, the departmental objectives and interim goals.

COMPETITION

Competitors are keen to get what you have—your job. If you don't show the company how much you're worth, they won't know it. If you don't learn how to compete, you'll never get to play the game as well as you can!

Competition is a reality of the work place, and always has been. It demands that you take advantage of any situation that falls within your circle of expertise and/or authority to make yourself stand out from the crowd.

Being client-centered, hard working and conscientious is all well and good, but if nobody knows how well you can perform vis-a-vis others in the company, your skills won't pay off as well as they can.

LEARN TO COMPETE

Wherever there's competition, there's risk. The person you are in competition with may be someone who doesn't believe in win/win positions. He or she may want you to lose. Yet, the team concept says that competition need not be about mortal combat, Iago-like deceptions or Machiavellian plots to take down a company.

If you can envision a win/win situation, your competitor may well be of a like mind and respect your ability to play the game.

I've found that many people have an uncomfortable relationship in competing with others, and suffer unnecessarily when competition comes calling. Snap! There's an emotional reaction when action in the name of self-interest—that is, a competitive stance—is required and they trip themselves up to lose or feel guilty if they win. Here then is a bare bones anatomy of how to quickly cure yourself of the fear of competition:

➤ **Don't take it personally.** In the film *A League of Their Own*, Tom Hanks, playing the manager of a 1940s all-women baseball team, gets nose to nose with one of the players who's fumbled a play and bawls her out about her ineptitude in no uncertain terms. She suddenly bursts into tears, to Hanks' great shock and horror, provoking him to scream more advice at her, "There's no crying in baseball!"

Like this supposedly toughened athlete, women tend to take competition more personally than men do. Sometimes we're moved to tears by a minor defeat, say, in a meeting or fall apart when we don't get a promotion. We feel "destroyed," "diminished," "humiliated."

These are overly dramatic assessments of an event and unproductive feelings about a temporary setback. That's all it is. Each time someone gets what you want at work or you're overlooked for the acknowledgment you need, congratulate yourself for the effort made. Remind yourself that you did your homework, you got into the fray, you tried your best—and didn't get the prize you sought. Do not flagellate yourself with unpleasant judgments about yourself. This simply reinforces the "personal" view of competition and makes it more difficult to get to the next face-off.

So, to paraphrase Hanks' baseball coach's wisdom, "there's no crying in business when you need to learn from your mistakes, gain confidence from the knowledge and get back into the game."

➤ **Hold your position.** If given the chance, a co-worker or two will happily roll right over you toward the corner office, and unflinchingly take the credit due you unless you hold tight to your position...and fight for it!

Not everyone plays fairly; you can always expect the expert on end runs to try and capture what's yours. Here's what I mean. You present a bright idea at a meeting and your supervisor jumps in, claims it as his and thanks you for bringing it up; a co-worker makes a joke at your expense about a personality flaw; another co-worker with whom you've created a sales plan for a major client excludes you when setting up a meeting with them.

Take my last example of the aggressive co-worker—call her "Sally"—seeking to make more points with the company and the client. Jane was the one pushed out of bounds. Here's the approach:

Although you, or Jane, can't change these appropriators at the gut level, you can hope to make them better competitors, especially when it's your neck on the line.

First, Jane has to be cool—no anger, crying or whining—and present her case to Sally.

Next, Jane must cover all the ground to protect her position.

She could say something like, "Sally, you did a good presentation of our sales plan at the department meeting, but we have been teamed on this project. It was my concept and I wrote the proposal. I don't appreciate how you went behind my back and excluded me from Friday's meeting. So, I've called our client to tell him how happy I am he liked the pitch and that we'll show together at his office on Friday.

We need to talk about how to work better together so there's no other misunderstandings. Lunch tomorrow?"

Jane was firm, made her point, set herself up in the meeting without looking foolish or denigrating Sally. Most important, she confronted the problem between them and suggested they meet to agree on a mutually beneficial remedy.

➤ **Know when to compete.** There are times when you may be a better coach or backup player than the star carrying the ball and should drop out to win! How? Acknowledge to co-workers that you want the team to win and believe your value is on the side lines, not the playing field.

A brief case in point: Willie, who is in your department and a second-tier manager, has a real gift for talking through objections and getting the sale. You are his manager and your strength lies in planning and analysis. Solution: When the situation calls for a personality with a dazzling sales gift, and it's not you, step back. Then suggest or promote a colleague who you know will get the job done. If it's Willie, who you think will get the contract or keep the account, let him do it!

Let yourself be seen as someone who wants the team to win, even if you have to pass the ball to a newer—more particularly skilled—player. Stepping back demonstrates that you're a wise competitor, a superior manager and judge. Such action can only add points to your scorecard.

➤ **Learn the plays.** If a quarterback called the signals in a huddle and none of his teammates knew what he meant, he'd be certain to set up a losing situation. The same is true in business competition—you must know what's going on in your industry, how it's expressed formally and in shorthand and what you need to know to rise in your field.

Since every industry has a terminology and a style of interacting, you do best as a competitor when the main players are clear that you know what they know—and that you say it in a rhythm and language that draws them in.

Back to "Willie" for a moment. Let's say he's the president of a theatrical production company; he wants to seal a co-producing deal with a hip film company, headed by an actor with big box-office draw. After he and his associate, Roger, meet with him and "his people," a summary comment like, "Sir, what I hear is that your three-year projection of motion pictures could feasibly be put into production with few serious financing restraints. It certainly fits well with our capabilities at this point in time...and, let me say this, we're looking forward to helping you implement your interim goals. Agreed, Roger?"

The actor/producer may go for such formal language and be impressed, but there's a good chance that he'd like Willie to level with him—as he's done—in an easier, conversational style that he can relate to and answer in kind. However, Willie would not need to change a word were he meeting with someone in an industry that rewards more formally presented plays.

Remember: Know the game and how to talk it. Don't speak in a manner that you expect will sound more authoritative to others. Financial people, lawyers and doctors sometimes fall into an excess of language to intimidate others, but it's not a good idea for you or me.

➤ **Cover your flank.** There will be those occasions when you are "beaned" by a colleague who rocks you on your heels by doing any or all of three things: 1) saying the wrong thing at the wrong time; 2) advancing a suggestion that is well-received moments before you are about to make the opposite recommendation and 3) equally distressing, nicking your credibility or reputation by giving you a "soft" introduction before you speak at a meeting or making an idle, or insulting offhand remark when you finish.

Competition is never so negatively charged as when you are "damned with faint praise," or simply undermined or attacked.

This can be touchy stuff. You don't want to put yourself in a position of making your colleague look bad in order to defend yourself—this brings you down to his level. One approach that works is to use a positive spin on a negative charge.

Suppose "Sally," "Jane's" rival, knows what she, Jane, wants to propose but speaks first at a meeting. Sally says, backed by data: "And so I think the company should divest itself of the XYZ division to decrease overhead and increase the bottom line..." Meanwhile, Jane was to propose a system to expand the XYZ division Sally recommends the company shut down.

Jane wants the board to go her way, but she has to defuse the impact of Sally's suggestion. This requires finesse and a remark like: "Sally can't know anything about this company or this business to twist facts like that! Plus, everything she says goes against all my research!" marks Jane as hot-tempered, if not unprofessional.

Instead, Jane gets the competitive edge if she detaches herself from her personal rivalry with Sally and sticks to the facts. Jousting with Sally makes everyone feel uncomfortable and steers them away from the goals at hand. She might say: "Yes, Sally's proposal makes short-term sense, but if we look at it from another angle, you'll see other options for not closing down XYZ. For instance— and let me pass this material out to all of you—my research shows that with expansion, we can eventually triple our profits. If you turn to page 3..."

Another action to take is to anticipate. Know who at your company is your lateral equal, someone with whom you share authority and/or someone who is working on another aspect of the job. Get together with him/her informally or send a memo—whatever your authority allows—then brainstorm and find out in advance what is on his/her mind. Especially if there is a meeting on the calendar.

If you know what your colleague is planning to say, you can present both options and both sets of data and work together as a team.

➤ **K.I.S.S.S.** This sibilant acronym stands for "Keep It Simple, Short and Specific." Although almost every situation you face in business can assimilate this concept, it is particularly useful when you are presenting a plan or strategy, orally or in writing.

Too often, we equate complicated and longer with being the better competitor. We figure we're the only one who understands the plan and wish we were indispensable— and so we make spiny and involved what should be smooth and brief. We toil over a 10-page report when a two-page summary with punch would be more effective. We add superfluous charts and footnotes to impress others, while a simple-to-follow table would do.

The truth is: If you're the only one who understands a plan or strategy, you go into battle alone! Exclude others by making them feel inferior to your report, and you can bet the plan won't be implemented. Know who you're dealing with and speak to them with intelligence and as equals, not as a grandstander.

BECOME VISIBLE

Toni Dewey, who is part of a group building a new "Women of the West" museum in Boulder, Colorado, told me that they chose as their logo the image of a circle with an abstract human shape and its shadow. I asked her why this design would typify the museum and its aims and she replied simply, "Because you must stand in the light in order to cast a shadow."

Her answer, of course, is both literal and metaphoric in meaning. To be noticed in the most pedestrian sense, one must be visible to others so they don't trip over you. But to be seen, to proclaim oneself, to be outstanding, one must seek the light so others are sure to single you out! In terms of succeeding in business, visibility deserves its own spotlight.

Before I look more closely at the "how-to" of visibility, let's start with an important "x" factor: your attitude about it.

Becoming highly visible for many people is a task that goes against their upbringing and conditioning. Here's where there's real separation between traditional lessons on being good little girls and good little boys.

In the briefest summary of outmoded and antiproductive thinking, most little girls are taught that modesty, downplaying their accomplishments and taking second place gracefully are virtues to be cultivated to the grave. We can safely say that Madonna, for one, never listened to poor advice about visibility and its relationship to career advancement. Little boys are given much more of a break, if not taught to exaggerate accomplishments and appear to be more than they are to a girl's being less.

In either case, becoming visible involves exposure and risk.

If you are interested in career advancement, keeping yourself a secret keeps you in the same place.

"Visibility is often what makes the difference between dramatic professional success and average achievement," wrote authors Dawn-Marie Driscoll and Carole R. Goldberg in their book, *Members of the Club: The Coming of Age of Executive Women.* "Substance and achievement are valuable, but they are less so if only a supervisor knows about them...Effectiveness in the Club demands a personal dynamism that commands attention, respect and admiration. This is true for everyone..."

There are a few key points you should know about visibility to help you understand its place in the course of your career: where to become visible and how to do it.

The where is usually clear: within your company or within the marketplace. The effort you'll make to be noticed and how you use your skills for advancement at your present job and where you want to eventually rise to are slightly different. In terms of lifetime employability, they are both quite important.

Getting noticed by your supervisor, or the company CEO or the vice president of another company where you see yourself in the future takes time. Let's start at your present place of employment. You want to become visible...to get the perks, the promotions, the raises, the rewards of hard work, access to power—whatever it is that you seek. So you venture out, take a stand, make a pitch, do the reports, speak at the meetings, and no one is interested. This is the worst-case scenario, but that's okay. Every star—in any business—started slowly and was first heard by a very small audience.

If there is a rule for you to remember, it's that becoming visible is a slow process.

"Maybe you can't help getting noticed where you work, but what about getting to 'the names' in the business? It's all connections, isn't it?" a rather frustrated and disgruntled menswear salesman at an upscale clothing shop asked me. He was trying to get an interview at one of the big designer houses and so far had no success."

"Who do I have to know?" is a question I hear frequently when it comes to visibility. I was speaking to Los Angeles management consultant Tom Drucker about this issue and he told me:

One of the things that's changing is the "old-boy network." Historically, people thought that to get ahead, you had to kiss up. Know the right person. Relationships are still important, but what's more important is your ability to accomplish things. The equality around results will help anyone survive in a company, especially if they can also manage relationships.

This was advice I gave the menswear salesman—advice he took to his advantage. He had to understand that real visibility is a slow process that turns the light on you to by showing them how good you are, step by step—not necessarily who you know.

Personal power develops in stages, rule number two. It applies to how you show yourself at your company or in the marketplace:

➤ Make sure you receive credit for work you've accomplished—promote your positive qualities.

➤ Make sure everyone knows you're an enthusiastic member of the team.

➤ Innovate.

"Innovators are personal entrepreneurs, able to refocus the way they do things in response to a changing environment," wrote author Catherine D. Bower in *Working Smart* magazine. "Being an innovator means realizing there is more than one right answer, more than one way to solve a problem."

By going beyond your job description and devising fresh ways to help achieve company goals, you stand out. Submit plans to set up a new office, develop new procedures, suggest the names of or hire outstanding personnel, sell to people who haven't been sold to before. Of course, all innovation involves risk.

When you innovate, you openly reveal how you synthesize information and think. And while you sell you ideas, you're in the spotlight. There's the chance that your boss may dislike your ideas or find them unworkable; that's okay. What you've done is more important: You've shown him that you care about the job, the company and that you're tending your career. At the very least, he will know who you are!

TOOT YOUR OWN HORN

To make visibility more persuasive, to let others know who you are, don't wait to be nominated: Toot your own horn! One way to let people know what you've done is, as one advertising copywriter said, "practice talking in the spotlight and telling others how good you are."

When I mention the idea of self-promotion, often the reaction is, "Isn't that pushy, braggadocio behavior?" A research lab technician told me, "No one likes the guy who says, 'and then I single-handedly stopped the oncoming train...'"

As with anything in life and business, style and focus will make the difference. Practice in a little graceful self-promotion will soon get you in a position where you don't always have to tell people what you've done—your performance does it for you.

You don't want to steamroll people, unless you can do it with the humor and charm of heavyweight Muhammad Ali, who was always the first to tell you, "I am the greatest." Most people in the work world don't go around saying, "I should get the industry award for most brilliant vice president of sales this year," or "Did you catch how I turned the mutual fund market on its ear?" Hopefully, the evidence and the result of your work will precede you. It's there for all to see, but it doesn't hurt if you call attention to your accomplishments. In general, your efforts should speak for themselves.

But, wait. "Effort has to do with numbers," a mid-level manager at a pharmaceutical company said. "It's always how much and how many or how did you do? No one's interested in your philosophy of life!" When I asked George Haggerty, the consultant specializing in franchise businesses whether he thought "tooting your own horn" pivoted around numbers, he had an interesting take on the subject. He said:

> I think the best method of tooting your own horn is number crunching or singing your sales presentations or your sales results in numbers. In business, numbers are everything, but so are they in sports—you can't escape the fact that a number will tell how you're doing.
>
> In the arts, its probably appreciation and applause, but in mainstream business, you must be noticed some way. You can talk a great game in the locker room but out in the field, you'd better be able to cut it.

Is there some factor other than numbers for showing your individuality—making sure you stand out in your department or company? At some point in our career, we stop and ask ourselves, What am I good at? Is this my best work? How can I achieve greatness? How can I toot a better horn? I asked George Haggerty what he thinks about this. He added:

> You can be a great person since I believe there's something for everyone. You can be outstanding in your career, but you have to find your niche, one that need not have to do with statistics. You might be known for your ability to get along with people, or known for your work with a charity, or even known for your knowledge of Civil War battles.
>
> What makes you a human being, even at work, is that you're just not one-dimensional. If all you're known for is grinding out the numbers you'll always make an okay impression on people. I think you should tell people what's inside you, be willing to give of yourself and tell people how you feel and what you're interested in.

There's no better advice than this for tooting your own horn.

ASK FOR THE SALE!

A good salesperson knows that the sale isn't made until it's "closed"—until you get a yes or no from your client or customer. So many people are willing to stay in with a maybe, rather than collect a no and mistakenly feel rejected. A yes or a no is definite—maybe leaves you dangling in "maybeland," unless you attached a time limit to it.

And a good salesman is prepared to deal with whatever response is given. What I want to help you with specifically here is selling yourself (you're the product), asking for the job, the assignment, the bonus—whatever it is you want. It's all a matter of salesmanship.

Be prepared. Be thorough. Be confident. Now ask for what you want—and close "the sale" with a yes. In asking that all important question—"Then when do I start?" or its variation—you show you know what you want, you're specific and have the courage to ask.

Here are a few hints to help you get to yes:

> ➤ **Be clear.** Ask for what you want without beating around the bush or watering down your pitch with irrelevant issues. Don't distract your customer (your boss, would-be boss or

client) from your focus—making the sale/getting the job—by commenting on the wallpaper, the view from the office or how your shoes are fitting at that moment.

We tend to get edgy or agitated when the customer/ boss/client mulls things over, or looks distracted, though he's actually trying to figure out which way to go. Introducing another subject to entertain him, no matter how mundane, doesn't move him toward a decision in your favor; rather, you'll probably lose your sale.

Stay with the point of the sale.

➤ **Be direct.** "I think I could be the vice president of marketing," may sound like a statement of intent, but it's a statement without real power behind it. Where it fails is that it most likely won't accomplish its ends—getting you the promotion —because it sounds more like waffling opinion than a direct pitch for a job.

Ask for the job or the sale in a direct manner and back it up with reasons why "making the sale" would be mutually profitable. "I can bring 10 years of experience, the kind of innovative thinking you're looking for and an important contact list to this job," is more likely to get an interviewer's recommendation for your promotion to vice president of marketing. "I see you favor the line of separates in white and yellow—a great choice. We could ship 10 dozen in each color to you in three weeks. In fact, why don't we say, two weeks, and I'll write up the order," both concludes the decision-making process and asks for the sale.

➤ **Be calm.** Apologetic nervous giggles, distracting gestures, a stiff posture or tentative or strained inflection in your voice can disaffirm what you want to communicate. A customer/boss/client may misinterpret your personal uneasiness and negatively associate it with your product, rather than connect it to your nervousness.

Take a few deep breaths, cancel all thoughts of the other person intimidating you, think only of getting the sale and remember that you've done your homework and know your product.

➤ **Rehearse before you ask for the sale.** Sometimes the sheer stress of having to ask for a sale is enough to make you forget who you are and everything you know about the product. If you feel pressure like this, plan what you will say and do in advance. Sketch out a general character analysis of the person you're going to meet with—temperament, ambitions, likes and dislikes, whatever you know or can find out from others—and create a working, logical scenario for the two of you. Then enlist the aid of a spouse or friend, and play out the sale.

Let your partner play devil's advocate and raise objections, and generally be a hard sell. Figure out as many possible objections to buying you or your product as you can.

NETWORK! NETWORK! NETWORK!

Consider this:

Eighty percent of all people get a job through a "grapevine," or, more familiarly known to us now, a network. At first the number seems high, then when you think it through, the number makes perfect sense. Eighty percent of the population would not get their jobs through the want ads or a personnel office, but through a contact.

What power this mysterious interconnection has!

Networking is techno-speak for a process that has been known in the past as "being seen," "meeting and greeting," "schmoozing," and even "working a room." What it simply means is making a valuable connection with a potential client, customer, potential mentor, or linking up with someone who might be in a position to help you get the job you want.

People always tell me versions of how they have no network and prove their point by adding, "and I don't know anyone in one of the top accounting firms, which is where I'd like to be. So, how does someone with no power like me actually get to network?"

My answer is, think the rule of three. What do I mean? Like a human chain, you know someone who knows someone who can lead you to the very person, or the opportunity, you seek. Obviously, you must think about who to call first. If you wanted to contact, say, political strategist

James Carville to work with him on the 1996 elections, you wouldn't make your first call to a friend who's apolitical, who does no charity or public service work and never heard of the man.

Instead, you'd call a more likely person, someone more on the civic ball, who could give you three possible leads; from there, you'd call each of those contacts and get three more leads from each person—and so on, until you get your most direct connection to Carville.

The importance of contacts and the "rule of three" cannot be overestimated—it's a rule successful people use every day of their professional lives. What about the other side of the rule of three? You get the name and number of the person most likely to help you. Will he respond to you? In business, as in life, don't exclude anyone from your potential circle of contacts. It is an unwritten law in business life that no matter how harried an executive is, he is likely to take, or soon answer, a call or letter when a friend's or colleague's name is attached.

But there's more to networking.

Handing someone a business card at a cocktail party is not quite getting the most from the system, though it is a beginning. To be effective, networking should include a conversation to establish who you are, and a follow-up call, to acknowledge who they are.

The follow-up, let me stress this, is the second critical step for networking success. Many people who keep business cards make a habit of noting on the back of the card where they met the person whose card they're holding. Do the same.

If you don't have a business card file, start one to help you keep track of people going in and out of your life—at cocktail parties, seminars, adult education courses, professional organization meetings, backyard barbecues, even weddings. In the film *Working Girl*, Melanie Griffith and Harrison Ford, hot to put together a juicy merger deal, crash a wedding given by a hard-to-get-to money man for his daughter. Griffith brazenly cuts in to dance with the man, charms him and makes an appointment to see him at his office about her deal!

Impossible? Not really. A man running a huge money empire understands guts and passion—and why a woman would pitch the subject of mergers at a family celebration. Of course, she did it with grace and a low-key sales pitch, and it worked.

I don't recommend crashing parties, but I do suggest that you take a chance on connecting with the object of your search when someone in your network has told you exactly where to find him/her. It is then up to you to follow-up.

Follow-up is always to a specific contact and any reason is sometimes good enough to call. Maybe you met an insurance investigator at a seminar, who mentioned that he liked mystery stories. You're interested in getting into his specialty and give him your card after his talk. A week later, you see an article about the 1940s "dime detective" magazines that have pretty much disappeared off the stands, and send it to him with a note, reminding him of how you met. If he doesn't send a thank-you note or call, touch base with him. In a brief conversation, bring up the article, let him know you're interested in his field and ask if he has any suggestions for you—then, if he sounds amenable, make an appointment for lunch or a drink.

If he says no, find out why not and come back with a different plan. If he says yes, be clear about what you want to do in his field of insurance, be clear about what plan of action you think might help you get into it, and how he may steer you to your goal. Be sure you know what you want to happen because of this contact. Don't hesitate to ask for what you want; it's pointless to hope the contact will offer it to you. He will respect you for being direct and asking, rather than being manipulated into making the offer.

You don't want to leave a valuable member of your network with the feeling that you are out to manipulate them. Whatever your reason, don't leave them hanging on trying to figure out what you want. Calling back repeatedly hoping they'll guess is the fastest way to lose an ally.

Continuance further develops the idea of follow-up. With continuance, you keep in touch and cement relationships. It offers the chance for you to nourish others' confidence in you and what you can do by being understanding, helpful and interested in him/her.

Business relationships, no different than personal ones, thrive or wither according to what you put into them. To survive, they need constant tending, support and communication. It's a good idea, then, to contact each member of your network at least once a year. Before you dial, try to recall what you talked about last. Many people keep a diary and jot down a few notes about the key issues in each person's life. Were they in the middle of a big deal the last time you spoke? Ask them now how it went.

Often, many of the people you "know" you only know by phone, especially if they're in another city. Contact them in person when you can. When you travel, always check to see who you know in that location and can call to meet—that is, the people who were not on your business priority list. Call in advance to let them know you'll be in town and set up a date, if you can, to meet for coffee. It often means a lot to people that you made an effort to see them.

There is only one caution in any request you make to someone in your network: be reasonable. Your contact isn't meant to do your work for you. They can provide an opportunity, needed information or a valuable lead, but you must be your own agent.

In understanding the function of a networking connection in terms of employability, be sensitive to what their schedules are, and how much time they can give you. An unreasonable push can turn the tables on you, as with Sarah George,* a financial analyst with a specialty in the European market.

Sarah had a masters in economics and had two years of work experience when she fortuitously met a man who could steer her toward a plum company, and a possible job utilizing her skills. Sarah first talked to Bob at a huge Christmas open house where the hosts were mutual friends; the informality of the occasion and Bob's natural good will encouraged Sarah, especially when he suggested she send him her resume. She told me:

> Bob suggested that I send him two copies of my resume, and that he'd send them out to the "right" people. Of course, I got excited that someone with his power would help me. So I called him a two weeks later, and he said he'd get back to me. Then I heard from our mutual friend that he was in the process of closing down two of their branches and laying off about 2,000 people.
>
> So I waited another two weeks, and called him again and asked him if the resumes had gone out and why no one was calling me! Was he helping me or not?
>
> Finally, I called Bob twice more, and got no return call. Then it occurred to me that I'd blown it with Bob and been totally unprofessional.

While Bob opened up a network to Sarah by sending out her resumes, he offered no guarantees of a job for her. It was Sarah's responsibility to follow-up and call the companies Bob had generously contacted, and not sit back and feel entitled to a job. By her misdirected persistence and naivete, Sarah alienated Bob, an influential businessman and potentially long-term networking connection. If she'd been more sensitive to Bob's situation, she'd have understood the pressure Bob was going through in his company and not pushed her cause while ignoring his problem. In networking, giving means eventually getting. If your network has no reason to be concerned with you, unless you are interested in them.

FINALLY

Though we wish someone will come down from above and make everything right for us—hand us the great job, eliminate the competition, give us access to power by making us the pivot point in a huge network, make it possible for others to remind us how indispensable, skilled and brilliant we are—alas! such magic will probably not bestowed on us. However, we have the ability to make some of this happen for ourselves, step by step.

Assess your career objectives. Assess the qualities you have that can move you ahead to success—and give yourself permission to have a great time at it, too. After all, the very worst thing they can say is no—and then you can find out how come.

WRAP-UP

➤ You must know your career mission so that you can build objectives, set goals and get out there!

➤ To insure lifetime employability, understand that everything that goes on around you in business can influence your future. Every meeting, every networking opportunity, every day you work, there exist opportunities to secure information to help you set new goals or adjust old ones.

➤ Goals should be specific, achievable and consistent with your personal life plan. Big goals with large numbers sound good, but you must have a reasonable and do-able plan to get you what you want.

➤ Keep your goals realistic. Remain flexible about how to achieve goals, review your goals periodically in light of new information and make sure your goals don't conflict with the mission of the goals of your employer, clients or customers.

➤ Learn to compete. Wherever there's competition, there's risk.

➤ Know when to compete: There are times when you may be a better coach or backup player than the star carrying the ball and should drop out to win!

➤ K.I.S.S.S., or "Keep It Simple, Short and Specific." Although almost every situation you face in business can assimilate this concept, it is particularly useful when you are presenting a plan or strategy, orally or in writing.

➤ Become visible. This involves exposure and risk, but If you are interested in career advancement, keeping yourself a secret keeps you in the same place until retirement.

➤ Visibility often makes the difference between dramatic professional success and average achievement.

➤ Personal power develops in stages—don't give in to modesty. Make sure you receive credit for work you've accomplished, promote your positive qualities and make sure everyone knows you're an enthusiastic member of the team and most of all, innovate.

➤ Make visibility more persuasive and let others know who you are and toot your own horn! One way to let people know what you've done is practice talking in the spotlight and telling others how good you are.

➤ Ask for the sale! A good salesperson knows that the sale isn't made until it's "closed"—until you get a yes or no from your client or customer.

➤ Keep expanding your network! Eighty percent of all people get a job through a "grapevine," or their network.

➤ Business relationships, no different than personal ones, thrive or wither according to what you put into them. For a network to survive, they need constant tending, support and communication.

8

SPECIAL ISSUES: IF YOU'RE OVER 40 OR TECHNO-PHOBIC

---

arlier in this book, in Chapter One, I recounted a talk I had with a Bostonian woman who left her job at a floundering advertising agency and was considering where to move next. When I asked Dee for her opinion about staying employable into the future, she said, "generally, learn the computer and never grow old." She never thought her off-hand remark would come back to haunt her. But it did.

After appraising her skills, thinking about where she'd want to work after the agency—and mostly, how she could best spend the next decade or so transforming her career—Dee came to a conclusion that stunned her: She'd go into desktop publishing, which meant she had to learn computer skills and a number of software programs.

I asked Dee how she came to desktop publishing. "In a way, I had no choice," Dee said, and continued:

> I never thought of myself as smart with machines. In fact, they scared me. I'm not very dexterous or coordinated—I can manage a toaster, but forget anything more complicated than an on-off switch.

Then when I had to make a decision about my life and my career, I had to grow up and face a few truths. Desktop publishing transferred to the kind of work I wanted to do, and my age wouldn't be a factor in getting hired. I signed up at a "user friendly" computer school and took a few intensive courses and learned the programs.

There's hope for people like me.

Daily events in the world reminded Dee that the Information Superhighway was not a far-flung concept. Personal adaptation to technology is no longer left to the specialists or brain trusts—even a kindergartner can learn a video game or a simple program in a short time. Technology isn't just serious business any more, it's everyone's business.

Arnold Brown, the New York futurist and consultant, is sympathetic to Dee's case as more men and women like her switch focus from using the computer as an incidental office appliance to making it a pivotal tool. However, he thought mastering the computer wasn't as important as what it provides us. He told me:

Anybody can run a computer, and in the future, even idiots will be able to use them—they'll be so easy.

But we don't have to teach people how to use computers, we have to teach them how to use the information that computers generate, and that requires communication and sharper analytical skills.

Of course, he's right, especially when we consider that there has been more information produced in the last 30 years than during the previous 5,000. And the information supply to us doubles every five years. Once we were a nation that complained of the piles of newspapers and magazines that didn't get read. Now all the computer networks can store and disseminate even more information. Will it overwhelm us? How do we handle it all?

WHAT TECHNOLOGY AND INFORMATION IS TELLING US

While the popular romance novelist, Danielle Steele, is rumored to still write all her chart-burning books on the Royal manual typewriter she got in college, and hasn't even graduated to an electric model, ignore people like her. Don't look to successful Industrial Age examples

---

Techno-Shock and Techno-Miracle:

➤ A weekday edition of *The New York Times* contains more information than the average person was likely to come across in a lifetime during 17th century England, wrote Richard Saul Wurman in *Information Anxiety*.

➤ If you're in Paris and you decide to use your American Express card, getting credit approval involves a 46,000-mile journey back and forth over phones and computers. The job can be completed in five seconds, wrote Peter Large in *The Micro Revolution Revisited*.

---

to defend your ambivalence about learning your way around the computer in your office.

Becoming satisfied with what you knew yesterday may be the quickest way to make yourself obsolete—unless like Steele, you can make millions of dollars a year, your way.

If we've learned anything in the 1990s, it's that we have to approach information objectively, as objectively as we approach technology itself. Most of us are very subjective about information and tend to over identify with facts, and pick out what refers to us.

To plan for your own long-term employability, be aware of changing marketplace requirements and remain flexible in your response to them. We have to expand our interests and increase our techno-skills— we have no real choice!

WHERE TECHNOLOGY IS LEADING US

Technology has insinuated and ingratiated itself into all phases of management, affecting all skill bases. Can you imagine life without computers, or CD-ROMs, data bases and all the other technological wonders we take for granted?

In the last seven years, "information receptacles"—like computers— in the United States increased by over 130 million units. *Fortune* magazine reported that Americans now operate out of 148.6 million E-mail addresses, cellular phones, pagers, fax machines, voice mailboxes and answering machines.

Fifty years ago, the simple computerized calculator that fit into the palm of your hand could only have been contained in the space the size of an airplane hangar. Twenty-five years ago, IBM invented the MagCard typewriter, the first typewriter to record on magnetic media. One card equaled one page. Now you can record 1,000 times that amount of information on a "card" half that size.

It has only been a little over 25 years that technology has driven the marketplace in such a dramatic scope. I think we can easily look, in part, to the space program and the astonishing technology that filtered down to us to apply in an everyday-usable way from those moon shots and space probes. Yet, the changes that have occurred and continue to occur because of it cut deep into what was once considered "doing business."

The old way of doing business was simple: You rented or bought a space and in that space, you set up an office. Your clients or customers came to this office to purchase your product or arrange for your service. Or, you sent agents or sales reps to your client's place of business, who took orders for your product and got it to them.

The telephone counted as the critical piece of technology; we awaited the mail delivery for payments by check, letters of confirmation or cancellation, an industry newsletter and more. Overnighting or messengering important documents was a common occurrence.

If you're over the age of 40, you remember such activities as part of a typical business day.

The new way of doing business involves an entirely new kind of "sales agent"—and technology plays a part of it pretty much across the board. Now, you need only set up a computer with a modem—a device used to send or receive information to and from your computer hard drive through the phone lines—install a FAX machine and buy a cellular phone and your office is anywhere.

You can query your potential or actual clients over a computer network "bulletin board," they can FAX their orders and then you can call your supplier and have the product shipped or call your service provider and have the client serviced.

Receptionist? A voice mail—or telephone answering device—takes your calls.

Secretary? A word processing software package may not type the information into the computer, you do; an electronic printer "types" your letters. Software will spell check, grammar check and, if you go more sophisticated, allow you to design the page and even your company logo on the stationery.

On the road and need to check a report? Just flip the on switch on your portable lap top, and, as they say, "interface."

"As technology permeates work life, assumptions about career tracks are turning upside down," said *Business Week*. Almost an understatement. The changing marketplace, driven in part by increasing technological sophistication, has made the world smaller, made information flow faster, increased the amount of information we must know—and increases our productivity. Technology has changed managerial functions and corporate structure and reduced the amount of office space needed to house it all.

Problem-solving, production, staffing—in fact, anything that has to do with business today is being touched by new ideas, much of which are directed by modern technology. Here's more of what the simplest office PC can do for you:

➤ Since you want to increase your employability, ongoing, continually updated knowledge of modern technology is a key selling point—even for mid- and upper-level managers. Computer know how is the most transferable of skills in the marketplace.

➤ You should be able to access the information you need, at any time of day or night, without having to worry if there's a "tekkie" around to do it for you.

➤ Technology is your friend: It allows you, for example, to pull up the history of your customers or clients—even the way they pay their bills—by hitting a few key strokes. As you add to your customer or client base, you can have the machine sort them according to your rating system. And you always have an updated mailing list.

➤ If you work in a small business, technology can make your company appear larger. You can keep a limited inventory in your office, mostly for sales presentation purposes, but fill complicated orders by interfacing with your warehouse computer, or simply faxing the warehouse supervisor.

➤ If you so think it, technology is an equalizer. Harriet Rubin, executive editor at Currency/Doubleday in New York said in an interview in *Inc.* magazine, that...

> Technology doesn't get enough credit for being the feminists' friend. Technology has killed hierarchy. When you get into companies that have E-mail systems, you don't have to be the loudest man or the biggest braggart. It flattens gender differences.

➤ And the big reality: Technology will soon affect every part of the marketplace, including your job and career.

Small Business Loves Technology

Small business owners rate information technology as a major factor in making their companies work faster and smarter—and there's no turning back. The "little guys," says *Business Week*, "are rushing into the Information Age." In fact, computer makers cite small businesses as the next great untapped market, after home PC users.

It has not been even 15 years since computer language compatibility became a factor, but now you speak without thinking about what disk operating system your particular computer uses. In the not-too-distant future, today's uncommon piece of office equipment will become tomorrow's common appurtenance, like video phones for teleconferencing, using television screens an inch thick that will hang on the wall—not even take up counter space.

Computers are already off the assembly lines that respond to all manner of input devices, including the human voice and human touch. You don't even have to know touch typing or even the hunt and peck system on a keyboard. You just need be able to speak into a microphone, as if you were giving dictation.

YOUR PLACE IN THE TECHNOLOGY

The Harvard Business Review noted that the "painful upheavals in so many companies in recent years reflect the failure of one-time industry leaders to keep up with the accelerating pace of industry change. Any company that is a bystander on the road to the future will watch its structure, values and skills become progressively less attuned to industry realities."

In large part, being attuned to industry realities is honoring what technology can do. You don't have to like it—just use it.

The success of the information superhighway depends, in its way, on you. To simply learn how to work a word processor or use digital equipment is not enough to help you stand out as an asset to your company.

The question runs deeper: How does a particular technology add value to your company? And which technology? Think about ways in which it can make you and your department more productive and take you and your company to meet its upcoming challenges.

In gearing for the future, think what changes you can help implement to solve a problem. People who remain employable learn how to rethink "core concepts," such as customer base, product delivery, competitive advantage and executive requirements.

Janice Riley*, a 28-year-old invoice project manager for a large manufacturing company involved in computer equipment, spoke with me about "competitive advantage" in this fast-moving decade. She thought that while knowing the computer is helpful, good business sense and understanding the industry you're in was equally as important. She said:

> After all the cutbacks and downsizing, I think the people who remain in a company will have to have softer skills. By this I mean a broader perspective of processes, an ability to integrate things, real value-added type of judgment and customized solutions. I think that in some cases, people obsess over the technology and don't bother to get good training or experience.

Janice works with a man she thinks is the perfect colleague. Chuck* is 32 years old and vice president in Janice's department. What impresses her about him, she said, is that he always questions why things are the way they are, no matter what or who generated it. Her comments confirms Arnold Brown's thesis, mentioned earlier, that how you use technology—analyze it—is what counts. Janice explained:

> Other people may say, that came out of the computer, that's all we have. But Chuck really looks at it from different angles. He'll understand the different systems, figure out the possibilities and flexibility that each system has and what exceptions can be made.
>
> And if something can't be done in the system, it can be done by hand and worked into the system at a higher level.

The thing about Chuck is, he's always going to find solutions that nobody else can. He's going to thrive.

How can technology help you take advantage of the future, rather than being an impediment to it?

Ask yourself:

➤ In which direction is my company headed?

➤ Does my company have a plan to utilize technology in the future?

➤ What opportunities does this open up and how can I take advantage of them?

➤ Do I have skills for the future, and if not, how do I acquire them?

➤ How do I want my skills in technology to augment my skill base?

➤ What else do I need to know to best sell myself and remain employable?

THREE REASONS THAT TECHNOLOGY IS YOUR FRIEND

➤ **It provides a fast and easy way to network.**

In the mid-1990s, business spent approximately $14 billion in networking software and hardware.

Why? The information structure no longer operates vertically. When it did, information was passed within one department up the ladder of responsibility to the next person who decided what application the information had. Then it was passed on to whomever was finally responsible for acting on it, one way or the other.

Networking now is all about the lateral distribution of information. If Joe, in Shipping in California, has a problem with Bob, in Receiving in Dubuque, Joe doesn't contact his supervisor. Instead, he gets on the "net" and contacts Bob directly and works out the problem.

If you're a manager seeking to keep your department running smoothly, change your focus from managing and passing on the information—to facilitating action. Get in the know about your company's networking capability and use the net yourself. It can only increase your ability to manage successfully.

➤ **Your specialty may soon be on a data base. Connect in.**

If you work in a company that's not using data bases or word-processing software, you're in the minority, but not for long. Be the one to instigate change.

Familiarize yourself with what's coming off the line— go to a computer store and survey the field. What pertains to your specialty and can help your improve your skills on the job? Is it in the field of accounting, client tracking, sales statistics with a graphics package, taxes, spreadsheets, design graphics, architectural drafting, even desktop publishing. They're all out there, becoming improved every day.

You don't need a computer or knowledge of one to make your survey. Many computer software stores have demonstration packages they can pop in for you on the spot to let you audition the works. This kind of software survey can be of value when your company goes on line— and make you more visible as someone ready for the challenges new technology will bring.

If you commit yourself to achieving competency in this area, you can help lead your company into the 21st century, rather than follow.

> **Keep Up With New Standards of Doing Work.**

"Computers are like dogs: They know when you're scared of them." It's not an epigram, but a *Baltimore Sun* headline, probably voicing more than a few misguided opinions about computers.

Actually, computers, as we use them, only know what they're fed and can only give back what they've been storing. Of course, science is working on the manufacture of "artificial intelligence," or computers that think, even chat. Meanwhile, you're in charge.

If you're still techno-phobic after my enthusiastic encouragement to enter the 21st century on line, fight your fear. One way to get over it is the jump-into-cold-water approach: sit down at the keyboard, hire an expert for a few hours to start you off on how the software works and learn it, a bit at a time.

It can only add to your global knowledge and demonstrate your willingness to learn. A computer is a tool like any other. Manage your attitude about technology and move into the future. Getting along with computers and a market that swears by them is simply a matter of learning how to "talk the talk and walk the walk."

WHEN YOU'RE 40 OR OLDER AND PONDER MID-LIFE JOB CHANGE

You may well retire and collect a pension without ever mastering office technology, but barring unforeseen circumstances, you will leave the work force, having reached the age of at least 40. Getting older is fate, getting more from work as you get older is your choice.

It's something to think about. In 1900, life expectancy was 47 years old, today, it's 76. In the next 35 years, one in five Americans will be at least 65! The 1992 Bureau of Labor Statistics Report showed 15.4 million Americans 55 or older still in the work force and that figure will grow by 38 percent by 2005.

So we'll probably be older, and working—but what is it like for the over-40 employee now and what can it be like for you? This touches on a number of practical and sensitive issues:

When we're 22 and starting out, the numbers that interest us most involve income. Very few of us think about hitting a plateau at 40 because the company we work for is unable to promote up any longer. Or of aging—and a mid-life job or career change at 50—and certainly not retirement at 65. Back then, starting out, our gazes are fixed upward, to more and better.

As I've noted throughout this book, the nature of success is no longer defined by the concept of going "up a ladder." The shape of work no longer follows one foot after the other, but may take form by moving to "musical chairs" and/or a "two step." So after 25 years of experience in the work place, more or less, it's possible that your career will change course—to your surprise or chagrin and against your will. Or your career can change course and fulfill new career goals—if you are ready to face the inevitable, plan ahead or plan smart.

In talking to people over 40 across the country about staying in or moving on, here's what I found to be a few of the issues and problems they've confronted. Let's take it in the "bad news-good news" frame of reference, starting with:

THE "BAD NEWS"

> ➤ Since companies, especially the larger ones, are pulling layers out their structures, there are about 50 percent fewer job openings at all levels now than there were in 1985. Some flattened organizations are broad benting, or rewarding people with raises unaccompanied by promotions. The virtue of broad benting is that the more skills you acquire, the more you may earn, albeit without a better title.
>
> Which brings us back to the issue of cutbacks, especially in large organizations for the over 45-year-old worker: you've got a good chance at being downsized out unless you have an usual skill or a reputation that pulls in business. Most of us aren't going to be hired at 50-plus at a large corporation—and you're right, it's ageism. Most corporations will deny it, but I think age discrimination is at work for a number of reasons:

1. You cost too much. Your salary is higher at 45 than it is for a 22-year-old coming in to take over your job. The health insurance actuarial charts aren't your friend, either. The premiums go up the older you get; the charts say you can get sicker more seriously at 45-plus than at 25 years old, and your company doesn't want to pay the bills. Statistics seem to say you can be a burden, no matter how you argue that you haven't been ill since you were 25.

2. Large companies tend to believe that older employees are not as adaptable to change, as trainable or as easily retrainable as a younger person. Actually, age has little to do with adaptability or trainability—it's temperament and the degree one takes risks that matters.

Resistance is more obvious in the older worker who may be made to feel insecure with change, and balks. But most people, young or old, are slow to adopt new ideas or shift points of view. Everyone wants to feel they are changing by choice, not by force. In fact, older workers are frequently the more productive than their younger counterparts.

By the way: I found that many people over 40 weren't as interested in risk taking as they were in getting a chance to be creative, to solve problems and make a difference. What they want from work, after all their experience, is gratification.

Questions You Must Ask Yourself
If You Are 50 and Older:

Know the answers to these questions if you are considering a mid-life shift in work or if you have been downsized into making the change:

What do I want from work at this stage of my life?

What do I need from work, in terms of money? Do I need to earn as much or can I afford a cut?

Do I require as much status—do I really need the big job at this point in my life?

How much ego is invested in my taking the next job? Can I scale down and do I want to?

AND THE "GOOD NEWS"

1. *Fortune* magazine reports that people between the ages of 36-60 are switching jobs in mid-life less often than they used to years ago. You may be among the people who are opting to stay in, finding ways to make peace with a job you may have outgrown.

So if your company hasn't downsized you out, you've still got some options: While employed, you can enhance your skills and explore what else is out there. What is this like?

"I've grown out of my job," Zach, a Seattle administrator, told me. He said:

> Frustration with routine is nothing compared to my being out on the street. I'm 52. What are my chances of finding a comparable job with a comparable salary?
>
> Right now, all I can do is look around the company and see if I can at least transfer into another department without losing seniority.

Like Zach, you could stay in and remain employable by plateauing productively—that is, look for opportunities to move sideways with no (or little) change in salary or title to a more interesting, or different department.

2. Other people over 40 can take a unique kind of chance: They leave a company and move down to a position in an organization that carries with it less power or a lower salary. But it's a job that can eventually offer more promise for the future.

3. Working for a large company is not the only answer to fulfilling work. If you have left a large company or want to, you may well find your niche in a smaller company.

Chances are good that you'll do well and be an asset to a small company—that is, with under 500 employees—or with a start-up group that has its financing in place. These companies need your expertise, your network, your skill base and your ability to adapt to change. What do you get?

You may be more on your own than in a larger company, and given more responsibility for a similar kind of job. They may not give you a health plan, and expect you to pay for one yourself, but you may be earning more. Or, if you're not hired, small companies will put you on as a regular outsourcer.

4. At 45 or older you're in a better position to relocate if a new job took you to another city. By your mid-40s, you should be more mobile; if you've got kids, they're either out of school or in college and not living at home. If they're still young enough to live with you, they can easily transfer schools.

If you own your own home, your mortgage is probably paid off, or close to it. Though you may be geographically attached to your present location, think about where you might want to be in 10 or 20 years—and look for a job there, now.

5. Entrepreneurial types will find their level when they switch jobs or careers and go into business for themselves. Lifetime employability also means that you can employ yourself.

How do you know if you are so inclined to running your own business? You've left clues along your career path, such as:

➤ You've always balked against the bureaucracy and done it your way.

➤ You've thought up new systems to increase profitability.

➤ You love making a deal.

➤ You've been a maverick in the organization.

➤ You keep thinking, "I'd like to run my own business before it's too late or I'm too old—but a business doing what?"

The answer is, look out there. You'll see old industries, struggling businesses, new industries, niche industries. Next, scrutinize your skill base. Your interests. Your networks. Put it all together.

I can't direct you to a precise business, but I can suggest you check out the real growth industries in the 1990s. They are in the accounting, distribution, production, marketing and human resource sides of food processing, education, medical technologies (including electro-medical equipment, surgical and medical instruments, botanicals and X-ray apparatus) and entertainment.

Also look the trends in the market. One such trend is the result of enormous cutbacks in non-profit and "do-good" areas, such as museums. These institutions have lost so much funding that they're making their money in marketing—that is, through museum stores. Such stores have become a big growth industry across the country as stand-alone retail shops selling reproduction jewelry, dishes, statues, posters, games, children's toys and more.

MAKING CHOICES: ONE DISCOVERED, ONE FOUND

Of course, your interests and skill sets may suit other industries or niche markets. I spoke to two exceptional people who have both opted for a niche in the entrepreneurial path. The first is a woman who has always been an innovator and an original and the second, a man who comes from a linear career path in the armed forces.

What was most fascinating about Elaina Zucker, was that she'd come to a crossroads in her work life and didn't know what to do next. This surprised me because Elaina, now in her early 50s, was always so in control of her career. She has an illustrious resume, including work in the fashion area, marketing and publicity; she's written books on leadership, been a seminar leader and, along the way, ran a singles organization.

A master in all aspects of communication, Elaina even went back to school to qualify as an organizational development specialist. She recently moved to the west coast, and ready for a new life, she's stuck! So while she's sequenced her careers in a way that makes sense, now she doesn't know what to do...next.

What I did to help Elaina was to gather at my house ten of her friends who knew her best and arranged an evening called, "Reinventing Elaina." Basically, we were to look at all the things that Elaina had done in her life, what she may want to do and, synthesizing that information, come up with a number of career possibilities for her. Elaina said:

> I could listen to everyone, but the hard part was that I could not speak, other than to say, "uh, huh," "tell me more" or "I never thought of that" I'm a very gregarious person and it was difficult just to listen!
>
> On my side, I came prepared. Carole gave me an assignment that began a month before the meeting. It consisted of thinking what I'd like to do, writing it down on a slip of paper and dropping it in a shoe box by my bed. I had to do this every night before I went to sleep for 30 days.
>
> I wasn't allowed to review my ideas until the last day, or one day before coming east. Then I made a list of all my career "ideas" which I would present at the meeting.

So we heard Elaina out—then she had to remain silent—while we discussed her skills and competencies and gave her examples of them.

We concluded that Elaina was the following: great at brainstorming, at going beyond boundaries, creative, resourceful, conceptual, original and a good synthesizer. She's also a risk taker with a lot of chutzpah, she's great at sales and a good networker.

We looked at her hobbies and passions, incidental interests, and we concluded about Elaina that she loved talking, art, shopping, exotic travel and exotic food. But Elaina was aware of all these qualities and told us, "I know all this and I still don't know what to do."

Then one friend brought up a quality Elaina didn't know she had and it amazed her: She was a wonderful collaborator. She said with great animation, "Tell me more!" The eleven of us provided her with chapter and verse on how she was a good partner and could form a partnership if she so chose.

Elaina has always been a loner or in business for herself, so the idea of joint venturing was a new concept for her. And in what kind of business could she joint venture? We came up with these suggestions, ideas she'd never considered: a movie or a theatrical producer, a literary agent, a deal maker, a television show hostess, a representative of the arts, an advice columnist or a licenser.

She synthesized the information that came out of "Reinventing Elaina" evening...and reinvented herself. Her new career is this: She's collaborating with a psychotherapist who has a fine reputation in the singles area. "Singles" issues are, in fact, part of her background, since she ran a dating service years ago and wrote a book on leadership and personality types.

With this therapist, Elaina is creating a theatrical and psychotherapeutic experience—"self-help" evenings for singles, which she will produce and he will direct. Using improvisational actors along with the audience, they'll do improvisations of how people act on dates and how they relate to one another, followed by discussion groups.

For Elaina, it's the perfect niche market in a collaborative effort.

For Gary Daniel Hartsock, chief of a performance team, and a civilian working for the Armed Forces and in charge of closing the army ammunition distribution centers, a mid-life career change is a bit different.

Now in the third round of closing the defense centers, Gary's seen personnel cutbacks from 26,000 employees in 1990 to 19,000 in 1995; by 2001, just a few years away, there will only be about 6,000 people left.

So, here's Gary. At 48 years old, he figures he's got about two years remaining before he's let go since, he says, "they're even getting rid of one-star generals." As with a for-profit large organization, armed forces downsizing means some people are pensioned off, others are given early incentives to leave, some are given severance pay in a lump sum—and there are counseling services available.

For many people with his experience after a downsizing, they tend to go into warehouse, security or consulting jobs in the private sector. Gary said of one such case:

> I was friends with a one-star general who was forced to retire at 51 and who went into consulting work in transportation. The thing about this guy is that he understood everything about accounting with the government since he'd done it for 30 years.
>
> He went to a top civilian accounting firm which wanted to get certain government contracts. In order to get them, the firm needed someone like this general who understood how government accounting systems worked.

The general helped the firm get their proposals through, and they paid him a high hourly rate as a consultant. Now he's working 20 hours a week and earning nearly double the $90,000 he earned as a one-star general. Gary said of him:

> What he'd never realized until then was that the army was the world's greatest expert in technology, and he knew how it operated. Before, he had to deal with logistics for all the bases all over the world.
>
> All these other systems in the private sector were less complicated, so for him, it was simple coming in and doing one thing for one company as a consultant.

And Gary Hartsock himself? At the age of 48, he's preparing for the day he's let go. Given the projected statistics and being realistic, he knows it's in the cards for him. But he's not panicking, but planning for his future. He's putting away 10 percent of his salary every year, he has an investment account with the government and he's saving up for a down payment on his making his retirement dream come true: a small manufacturing company in South Carolina. He told me:

> I've always wanted a place on the beach where the weather's nice and I can run a small company, with maybe six to eight employees.
>
> I'm looking for a niche right now—looking to find a product I could make. Maybe it's a car part or something the market isn't providing. I'm looking forward to starting this business and being independent.
>
> I've been in public service for 25 years and no matter how high I could go, I'd still have to report to someone higher. In my own business, I won't have to answer to anyone else. I think my life at 50 will be a good life and the kids can come visit me.

Gary's not afraid of confronting the reality of starting over at 50—planning what he can, searching for a product and waiting for when the government offers him a package to leave, which he'll "grab."

FINALLY

Whether it's adjusting to the inevitabilities of the Information Age by accepting technology or believing you can always find the next career after 40—it's all in your attitude. If you feel you have to keep getting promoted up, you're going to short change yourself. To make a better career possible for you, put ego and status aside and ask yourself the really meaningful questions: What do I need in my work life? What is my life about now?

To stay employable and get more out of it, synthesize your skills, your interests and your dreams and find your niche.

WRAP-UP

> ➤ Personal adaptation to technology is no longer left to the specialists or brain trusts. Technology isn't just serious business anymore, it's everyone's business.

➤ In the last seven years, "information receptacles"—like computers—in the United States increased by over 130 million units. *Fortune* magazine reported that Americans now operate out of 148.6 million E-mail addresses, cellular phones, pagers, fax machines, voice mailboxes and answering machines.

➤ Technology has changed managerial functions and corporate structure and reduced the amount of office space needed to house it all.

➤ Problem-solving, production, staffing—in fact, anything that has to do with business today is being touched by new ideas, much of which are directed by modern technology.

➤ To remain employable, you must learn how to rethink "core concepts," such as customer base, product delivery, competitive advantage and executive requirements, in relation to how technology deals with them.

➤ Technology help you take advantage of the future, rather than being an impediment to it. Ask yourself:

In which direction is my company headed? Does my company have a plan to utilize technology in the future? What opportunities does this open up and how can I take advantage of them? Do I have skills for the future, and if not, how do I acquire them?

➤ In the next 35 years, one in five Americans will be at least 65! The 1992 Bureau of Labor Statistics Report showed 15.4 million Americans 55 or older still in the work force and that figure will grow by 38 percent by 2005.

➤ If you work for a large organization and you're over 45, you've got a good chance at being downsized out unless you have an usual skill or a reputation that pulls in business.

➤ Most of us aren't going to be employed at 50-plus at a large corporation—and you're right, it's ageism, though most corporations will deny it.

➤ Over 40 and still employed? Enhance your skills as much as you can and explore what else is out there. Plan your future now.

➤ You'll have a better chance of getting a job at a small company when you're over 40.

➤ If you want to go into your own business, go toward the growth industries or zero in on a trend.

EPILOGUE

If there's one single message I want to emphasize now that you've read *Lifetime Employability*, it's this: the only element of work that's predictable is the unpredictability of today's work place. It may sound contradictory and puzzling to figure out, but it's not. The outlook is good, your chances, better.

Today, you've got to think faster, work smarter and be reputably trustworthy. Business has about it a strain of "musical chairs"—the person you supervise today could be your employer five years from now! When you have a strong commitment to change and operate from integrity in how you work, not loyalty to whom you are working, you'll always achieve your career goals.

These may be "unpredictable times," but what's predictable is that we're in the knowledge economy. In order to keep up with it and thrive, you must be teachable! Seek coaches or mentors; talk to and listen to what other people have experienced and learn from them. Adapt to the times, work at your best and get the maximum satisfaction from work. And remember these points:

> ➤ Measure your success by how you manage, improve and enhance your skills and increase your knowledge.

➤ Give added value where you are working and stay as long as you are needed, and it is appropriate.

➤ Evaluate and rebundle your skills and knowledge so you can sell them with confidence within your own company or that next outside opportunity.

➤ Be adaptable and discard what "always worked before" if it is keeping you in the same place and not allowing you to keep pace with the times.

➤ Be a team player, but don't feel dependent on a single company—large or small—for lifetime employment. It is a concept of the past. Take charge of your career so you can always adapt or move on.

➤ Be aware of the new paradigm: we're no longer living in compartments, starting and ending our careers in the same kind of job with the same kind of duties. Once we were stuck in a little place where mastery of work brought us great boredom, something we confused with security.

Revitalize by expanding your universe. In today's economy and the work place of the 21st century, the skilled worker will have an ever changing repertoire. If you increase your skills with each job, you can only gain a sense of your own responsibility and win.

I am sure that if you're willing to accept what is, embrace change and are alert to where the horse is really going, then you'll find your way, and even lead others. When you take a path and are open to its twists and turns, you'll find you've accumulated experiences that will enhance the quality of your work life.

Philosopher Johann Wolfgang Goethe said, "Whatever you can do, or dream you can, begin it. Boldness has genius, power, and magic in it. Begin it now."

I wish you a beautiful journey.

CAROLE HYATT

RESOURCE DIRECTORY

When you begin to survey your market and/or to seek "members" for your network, you will need a starting point. One of the best starting points that the marketplace offers at the moment are multitudes of directories. Within each directory are specific organization listings, usually with a contact name. Often, the listings will also mention publications that the organization puts out, committees that you might be interested in serving on, and sometimes special awards and opportunities that the organization offers.

To determine what directories you may want to consult, you may want to first take a look at one of the directories of directories, amongst which is *Directories in Print.*

Directories in Print, 1995, 12th Edition. Terri Kessler Schell, Editor. Gale Research, Inc., Detroit, MI, 1994.

This publication contains 15,400 bibliographical entries of published directories worldwide. Entries are in 26 subject categories, as follows.

1. General Business
2. Manufacturing, Industries & Commercial Services
3. Construction Industries & Real Estate
4. Retail, Wholesale and Consumer Services

5. Banking, Insurance and Financial Services
6. Agriculture and Veterinary Sciences
7. Transportation, Utilities and Municipal Services
8. Management, Employment and Labor
9. Advertising, Marketing and Public Relations
10. Library and Information Services
11. Publishing and Broadcast Services
12. Telecommunications and Computer Science
13. Medicine
14. Health Care Services
15. Science and Technology
16. National Resources, Energy and the Environment
17. Social Sciences and Humanities
18. Education
19. Law, Military and Government
20. Community Services and Social Concerns
21. Associations, Philanthropy, Ethnic and Religious
22. Biographical and Genealogy
23. Arts and Entertainment
24. Travel and Restaurants
25. Sports and Outdoor Recreation
26. Hobbies and Leisure

A typical entry includes:

Name
Address
Phone

What the directory includes; what the entries includes; how they are arranged; frequency of publication; editors; advertising accepted; circulation; cost; fax number; and remarks.

Just to give you an idea of what you might find, I took the liberty of excerpting, and commenting on, some of *Directories in Print's* listings which I thought might be of specific interest to you. Although many of the listings include a purchase price, you can find most of these references at your public library.

If you're not sure consulting these resources is worth the effort, consider that just the listings noted below give you access to more than

162,642 listings of corporations, organizations and individuals who can help you stay employable.

American Directory of Job and Labor Market Information. Career Communications, P.O. Box 169, Harleysville, PA 19438. (No editor or phone listed.)

> This is a resource directory which provides "information on jobs and labor markets, including state and federal government personnel departments, job information centers, employment service centers, databases, libraries, and publications." Cost is $29.95.

America's Fastest Growing Employers. Bob Adams, Inc., 260 Center Street, Holbrook, MA 02343. Carter Smith, Editor.

> **Phone:** (617) 298-9570
> **Toll Free:** 800-872-5627
> If you're searching for a position in a growth industry, this directory may be just the ticket. It lists over "700 U.S. companies with at least 50 employees and a minimum growth rate of 20 percent over the last three to five years." Its latest edition is listed as the 1994 edition. It costs $30.00 in hardcover and $16.00 in paperback.

Researching Markets, Industries, & Business Opportunities. Washington Researchers, Ltd, 2612 P Street, N.W., Washington, D.C. 20007-3062. Walt Seager, Editor.

> **Phone:** (202) 333-3499
> **Fax:** (202) 625-0656
> Provides "lists of sources of business and market information" and then discusses "methods for studying markets and industries." Cost: $395.00.

Business Organizations, Agencies and Publications Directory. Gale Research, Detroit, MI, 1992. Catherine M. Ehr and Kenneth Estell, Editors. (I consulted the 6th Edition, but they are published yearly.)

> **Phone:** (313) 961-2242
> **Fax:** (313) 961-6083
> **Toll Free:** 800-877-GALE
> This directory contains over 26,000 entries concerned with United States business, trade and industry. Listed alphabetically under each general category, each listing includes the typical

information, but with one notable addition— the "top decision-maker".

Encyclopedia of Associations, 1995. Gale Research, Inc., Detroit, MI, 1994. Carol A. Schwartz and Rebecca L. Turner, Editors.
Phone: (313) 961-2242
Fax: (313) 961-6083
Toll Free: 800-877-GALE
The Encyclopedia lists over 22,000 Associations in the United States. All entries are listed under topics, so you must first consult the separate index to search for associations in a topic which is applicable and interesting to you and your professional expertise.

National Trade and Professional Associations of the United States, 29th Edition, 1994. Columbia Books, Inc., 1212 New York Ave, N.W., #330, Washington, D.C. 20005. John J. Russell, Managing Ed.
Phone: (202) 898-0662
This publication has been completely revised and up-dated yearly since 1966. The best thing about is that though the listings are all alphabetical, they are cross-referenced in five ways: (1) by Subject; (2) by Budget; (3) by Management Firm; (4) by Executive; and (5) by Acronym. Categories (2), (4) and (5) are unique and of particular interest. For instance: If you want to associate yourself with an organization that is budgeted at between $500,000 and $1,000,000 annually, you can turn to that cross-reference section and find only the names of those organizations which fulfill your requirement. Or, suppose, you've only heard an organization described as NAWBO or NAFE, you can turn to the acronym reference and look them up accordingly. Or, you may have met a network contact at a conference with whom you'd like to touch base. You've lost his or her card, but you remember the name. You can look it up in the alphabetical Executive Reference and find out what trade or professional association your contact is with! A really excellent resource.

Membership Directory of the American Economic Development Council. American Economic Development Council, 9801 W. Higgins Road, Ste. 540, Rosemond, IL 60018. Sheila Kerrigan, Editor.
Phone: (708) 692-9944
Fax: (708) 696-2990

Contains "approximately 2,300 member industrial and economic development managers, including executive directors of chambers of commerce; federal, state, and regional industrial organizations; transportation agencies, utility companies, banks, and others who promote economic and industrial development."
NOTE: THIS DIRECTORY IS AVAILABLE TO MEMBERS ONLY; however, if you are interested in this directory, you may also be interested in joining the AEDC, which, among other member services, offers a "rigorous, three-part certification examination" and career referrals. To receive a membership application or additional information about AEDC, you can write to them at the address above or call. Cost of membership varies from a $65 student membership to an "active voting member" price of $280.

Executive Employment Guide. AMACOM Books, American Management Association, 135 W. 50th Street, New York, NY 10020. Eileen Monahan, Editor.
Phone: (212) 903-7912
Fax: (212) 903-8163
Lists "over 150 executive search firms, personnel agencies, outplacement services, job registers, job counselors, resume writers, and pre-employment investigators" in over "140 job classifications." It is published monthly at a cost of $20.

Executive Recruitment Firms. JNN International, Inc., 6821 Sutherland Court, Mentor, OH 44060. Nayan Shah, Editor.
Phone: (216) 974-1959
"Published in 18 industry-specific volumes under the title, 'Executive Recruitment Firms Specializing in (industry name)'." Each volume may be bought for $7.00. It is published annually in September.

Standard & Poor's Corporation Records. Standard & Poor's Corporation, McGraw-Hill Financial Services, 25 Broadway, New York, NY 10004. Michael Antinoro, Editor.
Phone: (212) 208-8363
Fax: (212) 412-0459
This resource is continuing and served up in a looseleaf format. It is an excellent resource for basic company information. If you are going for an interview or meeting with a company for any

reason, this is a place to do some basic homework. S&P reviews over 10,000 publicly-owned companies. It is a service that must be subscribed to at a cost of $1,815 per year. Your library (or your stock broker) will have copies that you can look at, or, if you are online with DIALOG Information Services, Inc., Factset Data Systems, Inc., Citibank Global Report System, Mead Data Central or NewsNet, you can access these records through your computer. It is also available on CD-ROM for $4,900.

NOTE: Standard & Poor's, like Dun and other information services, publishes many and varied directories and resources. S&P's most famous is probably the *500 Directory*, which lists the "500 companies included in the S&P 500 Stock Index."

Career Employment Opportunities Directory. Ready Reference Press, Box 5169, Santa Monica, CA 90405. Alvin Renetzky, Editor-in-Chief.

Phone: (213) 474-5175

This directory is interesting in that it has separate volumes which list separate fields. There are four: "Liberal Arts and Social Sciences, Business Administration, Engineering and Computer Sciences, and Sciences." Published biennially, one volume may be purchased for $47.50 or for $190.00 you can by all four. (The price is slightly higher if you want them to bill you.)

The Consultants Directory of the American Consultants League. Kay St. Clair, Ed., American Consultants League, 1290 Palm Avenue, Sarasota, FL 34236.

Phone: (813) 952-9290
Fax: (813) 925-3670

The Directory is published every March, lists over 1,000 member consultants, and can be purchased for $30.00. An excellent starting point for those of you who are thinking of turning your skills and knowledge toward independent consultancy.

The Career Guide—Dun's Employment Opportunities Directory. Dun & Bradstreet Information Services, Dun & Bradstreet Corporation, 3 Sylvan Way, Parsippany, NJ 07054-3896.

Phone: (201) 605-6000
Fax: (201) 605-6911
Toll Free: (800) 526-0651

This directory includes more than "5,000 companies on leading employers throughout the U.S. that provide career opportunities in sales, marketing, management, engineering, life and physical sciences, computer science, mathematics, statistics planning, accounting and finance, liberal arts fields, and other technical and professional areas." Cost is $450.00 (lease basis.)

NOTE: Dun & Bradstreet is a well-known name in company information. One oft-used D&B resource is *The Million Dollar Directory*.

Executive Search Consultants Directory. American Business Directories, Inc., American Business Information, Inc., 5711 S. 86th Circle, Omaha, NE 68127.

Phone: (402) 593-4600
Fax: (402) 331-1505

This directory lists 5,457 entries compiled from the telephone company's "Yellow Pages." It can be gotten in hard copy, on disk, mailing labels, 3x5 cards, or accessed through Business American Online or DIALOG Information Services. It is published annually and costs $265.00 when paid with order.

NOTE: American Business Directories also publishes other specific directories compiled from the same source. A catalogue of all their available directories can be acquired for FREE, just by calling and requesting it. They also have other services which are less expensive than buying an entire directory. For instance: you can order short lists of industry-specific and/or state-specific firms that will be faxed to you at the cost of $1.00 per name.

Business Opportunities Handbook. Enterprise Magazines, Inc., 1020 N. Broadway, Ste. 111, Milwaukee, WI 53202. Michael J. McDermott, Editor.

Phone: (414) 272-9977
Fax: (414) 272-9973

If you're considering starting your own business, but are not sure which business suits your expertise, then this directory is for you. It lists "over 2,000 franchises, dealers, distributors, suppliers, and licensors offering business opportunities to individuals." Within each listing, it also notes how much money you'll need for start-up and whether "financial assistance and training services are available." It is published quarterly, at a cost of only $5.99.

NOTE: If you have a business opportunity in which you'd like to interest others, you can also advertise in this publication.

For Overseas opportunities, consult:

American Jobs Abroad, Gale Research, Inc., 835 Penobscot Bldg., Detroit, MI 48226-2094. Edward Knappman, Editor.

Phone: (313) 961-2242

Fax: (313) 961-6083

Toll Free: (800) 877-GALE

As we have noted, the new global economy favors those who have worked with, for or in other countries. This directory is an excellent source for those of you who want to "globalize" your professional horizons. It lists over "800 U.S. corporations and 100 government agencies, associations, and other organizations that employ Americans overseas, generally on an ongoing or long-term basis at wages or salaries comparable to those in the U.S." The price is $55.00. It's first edition was published in May, 1994.

Among other directories listed in *Directories in Print* which concern foreign opportunities are the *Business Researchers Euroguide* and *The International Business Directory & Reference.* There are also many country-specific directories, including Japan, Spain, Korea, Arab countries and South Africa. If you're sure where you want to go, then you might want to consult:

The Directory of Employment Agencies (Overseas recruitment). Overseas Employment Services, P.O. Box 460, Mount Royal, PQ, Canada H3P 3C7. Leonard Simcoe, Editor. (Distributed in the United States by EBSCO Industries, Inc., P.O. Box 1943, Birmingham, AL 35201 (205) 991-1330.)

Phone: (514) 739-1108

Lists "335 employment agencies in Canada, the U.S. and western Europe that specialize in overseas recruitment." Written in English, it is published annually and can be purchased for $15.00

Career Opportunities for Bilinguals and Multilinguals. Scarecrow Press, P.O. Box 4167, Metuchen, NJ 08840. Vladimir F. Wertsman, Editor.

Phone: (908) 548-8600.

Fax: (908) 548-5767

Toll Free: (800) 537-7197

It covers "3,500 companies and organization that hire people who are fluent in languages other than English." For those of us who are not already fluent, the directory also lists "colleges and universities, libraries, books and other educational resources for those wishing to learn other languages."

Executive Grapevine: The Directory of Career Management and Outplacement. Executive Grapevine International Ltd., 4 Theobald Court, Theobald Street, Borehamwood, Hertfordshire WD6 4RN, England. Robert B. Baird and Helen Barrett, Editors

Phone: 81 9539939

Lists "120 outplacement firms in the United Kingdom and Europe." It costs $50.00 and is distributed in the United States by Hunt Scanlon Publishing Co., Inc., 2 Pickwick Plaza, Greenwich, CT 06830 (203-629-3629)

NOTE: Executive Grapevine publishes a whole series of directories; not just the one noted above. Three others were listed in *Directories in Print: Directory of Executive and Management Development Consultants, The Directory of Executive Recruitment Consultants (United Kingdom), and The International Directory of Executive Recruitment Consultants.*

Independents who are looking for overseas opportunities might be interested in:

European Consultants Directory. Gale Research, Inc., 835 Penobscot Bldg., Detroit, MI 48226-2094. Karen E. Koek, Editor.

Phone: (313) 961-2242

Fax: (313) 961-6083

Toll Free: (800) 877-GALE

This directory lists approximately "5,000 consultants and consulting firms in Europe by subject." The most recent edition was published in 1992. It is priced at $250.00 and can also be purchased on disk.

European Directory of Management Consultants. AP Information Services, Roman House, 298 Golders Green Road, London NW11 9PZ, England. Alex Kaminsky, Editor.

Phone: 81 4554550

Toll Free: (800) 531-0007

Lists approximately "1,700 management consultancy firms in varying areas of activity and industry in western Europe." Published annually in May. The purchase price is listed as 120 British pounds.

If you want to get published, you might want to consult:

The Gale Directory of Publications and Broadcast Media, 1994. Gale Research, Inc., 835 Penobscot Bldg., Detroit, MI 48226-2094. Karen Troshynski-Thomas and Deborah M. Burek, Editors.

Phone: (313) 961-2242

Fax: (313) 961-6083

Toll Free: (800) 877-GALE

This publication "lists the name, address, phone, frequency, key personnel, and other pertinent information about 37,000 news-papers, magazines, journals and periodicals, and radio, TV, and cable stations and systems."

Of special interest to Women are the following:

Business Women's Network Directory. Kate Suryan, Editor. The Business Women's Network, Washington, D.C. 1994.

This is a brand new directory. It profiles more than 130 national and 270 local women's business and professional organizations, indexed by organization name and location. The directory was created as an effort to inform the growing cadre of women in business about what their fellow women executives and entrepreneurs are doing. Consequently, the profiles are detailed. A typical entry includes:

Leadership

Executive Committee

Organization Profile—a brief description of
the size, scope and history of the organization.

Focus Areas/Objectives

Membership Criteria

Membership Benefits

Local Chapters

Programs—a listing of what, when, where and who.

Meetings—a notation about who may attend.

Recognition and Awards—those given by the
organization

Education, Philanthropic and Community Commitments

Publications—not just a listing, but a description

Opportunities for Corporate Involvement

If you are interested in obtaining a copy of this directory, you may call The Business Women's Network at 1-800-48-WOMEN.

Resourceful Woman. Shawn Brennan and Julie Winklepleck, Editors. Visible Ink Press (TM), a division of Gale Research, Inc., Detroit, MI, 1994.

Resources are listed in this directory by area of interest, i.e., Aging, Arts, Community, Education, Global Issues, Health, History, Kinship, Politics, Sexuality, Spirituality, Sports & Recreation, Violence Against women, Work, and Youth. "Kinship" is a particularly interesting category, listing as it does references on organizations having to do with "birth, breastfeeding, rituals, contraception," and other exclusively female areas.

Resourceful Woman also includes a "selected list" of Feminist Bookstores across the United States where one can find the references and an index of all included organizations in alphabetical order.

Women's Organizations: A National Directory. Martha Merrill Doss, Editor. Garrett Park Press, Garrett Park, MD, 1986.

Though this directory is listed alphabetically, it has two cross-reference sections: by State and by Subject. This is particularly nice, if you just want to take a look at those women's organizations that have branches in your state.

NOTE: *Women's Organizations: A National Directory* and a special interest publication put out by Garrett Press entitled *The Directory of Special Opportunities for Women,* which includes educational, career, network and peer-counseling information, are out of print, but I was able to find them at the library. Garrett does have in print currently:

Women's Information Directory: Guide to Organizations, Agencies, Institutions, Programs, Publications, Services and other resources concerned with women in the United States, 1993 Edition. Shawn Brennan, Editor. Garrett Park Press, P.O. Box 190, Garrett Park, MD 20896.

The directory contains over 10,800 listings of organizations and services in 26 categories, including the top U.S. women-owned Businesses & Consulting Organizations; national, regional, state, and local women's organizations; and research and government organizations and agencies.

For Minorities, of special interest are:

Minority Organizations: A National Directory, Garrett Park Press, P.O. Box 190, Garrett Park, MD 20896. (I consulted the 4th Edition, published 1992. It is noted within the pages of the book, however, that this is an ongoing and continually updated resource.)

Organizations included in the Directory are listed for the following minorities: American Indian, Native Alaskan, African-American, Hispanic, and Asian-American.

Black Americans Information Directory. Gale Research, Inc., Detroit, MI. Darren L. Smith, Editor. (I consulted the 1st Edition, 1990-91.)

Phone: (313) 961-2242
Fax: (313) 961-6083
Toll Free: (800) 877-GALE

This directory contains listings for "4,500 organizations, Agencies, Institutions, Programs, and Publications concerned with Black American Life and Culture," including:

Associations	Newsletters & Directories
Awards, Honors, Prizes	Newspapers & Periodicals
Colleges & Universities	Publishers
Cultural Organizations	Radio & Television Stations
Government Agencies	Religious Organizations
& Programs	Research Centers
Industrial & Service Co.	Studies Programs
Museums	Videos

ABOUT THE AUTHOR

Carole Hyatt "walks what she writes." As an American in today's culture, she creates projects that integrate her varied background experiences in business, education and theater. Her activities include motivational speaking and interactive workshops on the international circuit. She travels regularly to five continents, speaking to audiences ranging from Jamaican women small business owners to Japanese multinational business professionals.

As a market and social behavior researcher, she has assisted Fortune 2500 companies, the media, and government agencies in creating hundreds of new products, programs and services. Her books, *Lifetime Employability, Shifting Gears, When Smart People Fail, Women & Work* and *The Women's Selling Game* are based on case studies of prominent and typical North Americans and have been reviewed as "seminal works."

Carole Hyatt has been on the faculties of The New School For Social Research, Hunter Graduate School, Woman's School, and New York University. She has lectured at Johns Hopkins University, Columbia Business School, University of Illinois, and numerous other universities and colleges.

As a career specialist, her speeches, lectures and books have one overriding design helping people get in touch with their natural gifts and skills in order to develop strategies for a fulfilling life.

Additional copies of *Lifetime Employability* may be ordered by sending a check for $12.95 (please add $2 for the first book, $1 for each extra copy, for postage and handling) to:

MasterMedia Limited
17 East 89th Street
New York, NY 10128
(800) 334-8232
(212) 546-7638 (fax)

Carole Hyatt is available for speaking engagements. Please contact MasterMedia's Speaker's Bureau for availability and fee arrangements. Call Tony Colao at (800)4-Lectur.

MasterMedia Limited
17 East 89th Street
New York, NY 10128
(800) 334-8232 *please use Mastercard or Visa on 1-800 orders*
(212) 546-7638 (fax)

OTHER MASTERMEDIA BUSINESS BOOKS

POSITIVELY OUTRAGEOUS SERVICE: New and Easy Ways to Win Customers for Life, by T. Scott Gross, identifies what the consumers of the nineties really want and how businesses can develop effective marketing strategies to answer those needs. ($14.95 paper)

POSITIVELY OUTRAGEOUS SERVICE AND SHOWMANSHIP: Industrial Strength Fun Makes Sales Sizzle!!!!, by T. Scott Gross, reveals the secrets of adding personality to any product or service. ($12.95 paper)

HOW TO GET WHAT YOU WANT FROM ALMOST ANYBODY, by T. Scott Gross, shows how to get great service, negotiate better prices, and always get what you pay for. ($9.95 paper)

OUT THE ORGANIZATION: New Career Opportunities for the 1990's, by Robert and Madeleine Swain, is written for the millions of Americans whose jobs are no longer safe, whose companies are not loyal, and who face futures of uncertainty. It gives advice on finding a new job or starting your own business. ($12.95 paper)

CRITICISM IN YOUR LIFE: How to Give It, How to Take It, How to Make It Work for You, by Dr. Deborah Bright, offers practical advice, in an upbeat, readable, and realistic fashion, for turning criticism into control. Charts and diagrams guide the reader into managing criticism from bosses, spouses, children, friends, neighbors, in-laws, and business relations. ($17.95 cloth)

BEYOND SUCCESS: How Volunteer Service Can Help You Begin Making a Life Instead of Just a Living, by John F. Raynolds III and Eleanor Raynolds, C.B.E., is a unique how-to book targeted at business and professional people considering volunteer work, senior citizens who wish to fill leisure time meaningfully, and students trying out various career options. The book is filled with interviews with celebrities, CEOs, and average citizens who talk about the benefits of service work. ($19.95 cloth)

MANAGING IT ALL: Time-Saving Ideas for Career, Family, Relationships, and Self, by Beverly Benz Treuille and Susan Schiffer Stautberg, is written for women who are juggling careers and families. Over two hundred career women (ranging from a TV anchorwoman to an investment banker) were interviewed. The book contains many humorous anecdotes on saving time and improving the quality of life for self and family. ($9.95 paper)

THE CONFIDENCE FACTOR: How Self-Esteem Can Change Your Life, by Dr. Judith Briles, is based on a nationwide survey of six thousand men and women. Briles explores why women so often feel a lack of self-confidence and have a poor opinion of themselves. She offers step-by-step advice on becoming the person you want to be. ($9.95 paper, $18.95 cloth)

TAKING CONTROL OF YOUR LIFE: The Secrets of Successful Enterprising Women, by Gail Blanke and Kathleen Walas, is based on the authors' professional experience with Avon Products' Women of Enterprise Awards, given each year to outstanding women entrepreneurs. The authors offer a specific plan to help you gain control over your life, and include business tips and quizzes as well as beauty and lifestyle information. ($17.95 cloth)

SIDE-BY-SIDE STRATEGIES: How Two-Career Couples Can Thrive in the Nineties, by Jane Hershey Cuozzo and S. Diane Graham, describes how two-career couples can learn the difference between competing with a spouse and becoming a supportive power partner. Published in hardcover as *Power Partners.* ($10.95 paper, $19.95 cloth)

WORK WITH ME! How to Make the Most of Office Support Staff, by Betsy Lazary, shows you how to find, train, and nurture the "perfect" assistant and how to best utilize your support staff professionals. ($9.95 paper)

THE LOYALTY FACTOR: Building Trust in Today's Workplace, by Carol Kinsey Goman, Ph.D., offers techniques for restoring commitment and loyalty in the workplace. ($9.95 paper)

DARE TO CHANGE YOUR JOB—AND YOUR LIFE, by Carole Kanchier, Ph.D., provides a look at career growth and development throughout the life cycle. ($9.95 paper)

BREATHING SPACE: Living and Working at a Comfortable Pace in a Sped-Up Society, by Jeff Davidson, helps readers to handle information and activity overload, and gain greater control over their lives. ($10.95 paper)

TWENTYSOMETHING: Managing and Motivating Today's New Work Force, by Lawrence J. Bradford, Ph.D., and Claire Raines, M.A., examines the work orientation of the younger generation, offering managers in businesses of all kinds a practical guide to better understand and supervise their young employees. ($22.95 cloth)

BALANCING ACTS! Juggling Love, Work, Family, and Recreation, by Susan Schiffer Stautberg and Marcia L. Worthing, provides strategies to achieve a balanced life by reordering priorities and setting realistic goals. ($12.95 paper)

STEP FORWARD: Sexual Harassment in the Workplace, What You Need to Know, by Susan L. Webb, presents the facts for identifying the telltale signs of sexual harassment on the job, and how to deal with it. ($9.95 paper)

A TEEN'S GUIDE TO BUSINESS: The Secrets to a Successful Enterprise, by Linda Menzies, Oren S. Jenkins, and Rickell R. Fisher, provides solid information about starting your own business or working for one. ($7.95 paper)

TEAMBUILT: Making Teamwork Work, by Mark Sanborn, teaches business how to improve productivity, without increasing resources or expenses, by building teamwork among employers. ($19.95 cloth)